DORSET SPORTING RUNS

DORSET SPORTING RUNS

RODNEY LEGG
IN COLLABORATION WITH
CHRIS COPSON

HALSGROVE
COUNTRY CLASSICS

First published in Great Britain in 2001

British Library Cataloguing-in-Publication Data
A CIP record for this title is available from the British Library

ISBN 1 84114 082 1

HALSGROVE

Halsgrove House
Lower Moor Way
Tiverton, Devon EX16 6SS
Tel: 01884 243242
Fax: 01884 243325
www.halsgrove.com

Printed and bound by The Cromwell Press, Trowbridge.

CONTENTS

	FOREWORD	7
Chapter 1	BECKFORD PERIOD	9
Chapter 2	STURT PERIOD	15
Chapter 3	MR FARQUHARSON'S HOUNDS	18
Chapter 4	MR YEATMAN'S HOUNDS	54
Chapter 5	MANSEL-PLEYDELL'S ROEBUCK HOUNDS	56
Chapter 6	THE MOUNTAIN HARRIERS	57
Chapter 7	THE PORTMAN HOUNDS	66
Chapter 8	CHARBOROUGH HOUNDS	74
Chapter 9	MR RADCLYFFE'S HOUNDS	80
Chapter 10	SOUTH DORSET HOUNDS	99
Chapter 11	BLACKMORE VALE COUNTRY	129
Chapter 12	THE RANSTON BLOODHOUNDS	166
Chapter 13	MISS SERRELL'S OTTER HOUNDS	169
	INDEX	173

'To every shrub the warm effluvia cling,
Hang on the grass, impregnate earth and skies;
With nostrils opening wide, o'er hill, o'er dale,
The vig'rous hounds pursue, with every breath
Inhale the grateful stream, quick pleasure sting
Their tingling nerves, while they their thanks repay,
And in triumphant melody confess
The titillating joy. Thus on the air
Depends the hunter's hope.'

Peter Beckford

FOREWORD

These are primarily huntsmen writing on hunting, through the best of hunting country during a golden age, mostly in their own words. Henry Symonds and Lady Theodora Guest have been our principal contributors from history. Wherever available, these and other contemporary descriptions and topography have been incorporated into the accounts, with only minimal editing. For consistency, and to aid identification, modern spellings have been applied to the placenames, though most remain unchanged. Some of the originals will fascinate local historians.

Running though these accounts is an appreciation and respect both for their quarry and the land they are crossing. The fox often came out at the end of the day in a better state than the horses, in the era when getting to the meet meant hacking there and no horsebox for the journey home, and the human participants had to be prepared to pay a physical price. Collectively the runs may be seen as a celebration of hunting but the object of the compilation has been to produce the first comprehensive Dorset history of a subject that has previously been sidelined into specialist publications. Many more such accounts languish in the files of the old broadsheet country newspapers.

The original post-medieval landscape comes through as an immense canvas, just about fully accessible to horse and hound – and for the fox to run away – before the natural barriers were reinforced by the nineteenth-century railways and twentieth-century motor cars. The other missing link, wonderfully absent before 1873, is barbed wire.

There was a sense of freedom in the historic countryside that comes across as exhilarating. Whatever your views about the subject – whether you are chasing with the hounds (Symonds) or running with the quarry (Legg) – it is a very different Dorset that we cover. There were still open sheep downs; functioning water-meadows; unenclosed common fields; and extensive heathlands where conifers now grow. Arable land was quite a rarity. Enjoy the landscape vignettes as well as the runs. Lament that the scenery, as well as the sport, has been marred by barbed wire, railways, tarred roads and suburbia.

Opening the story, for Dorset and the nation, is Peter Beckford. He is first and foremost, through having written himself a good press. Others, such as William Troyte-Bullock, who was Member of Parliament for Weymouth in 1768 and Shaftesbury in 1774, found sudden wealth and spent the rest of their lives on horseback. He took the name Chafyn-Grove upon inheriting Waddon House at Portesham and Zeals near Mere. Kennels for foxhounds were built at each property.

The bulk of our photographs come from the twentieth century, mainly having been taken by Weymouth cameraman Edwin Seward, and are reproduced courtesy of the photographic archive at Dorset County Museum.

Chapter One

BECKFORD PERIOD

PETER BECKFORD AT STEPLETON HOUSE

 When Thomas Fownes bought the manor and park at Stepleton House, between Shroton and Stourpaine, he proclaimed rights to hunt in Cranborne Chase. His pack of hounds was said to be the best in England. The house and kennels beneath the western escarpment of the Chase were sold in 1745 to Julines Beckford. His young son would become the great Peter Beckford (1740–1811) who, as a Dorsetshire gentleman, wrote his *Thoughts on Hare and Fox Hunting* at Stepleton. It is the first properly detailed account of the pursuit of hunting with hounds. He also wrote *Essays on Hunting* which had an introduction explaining how hares were hunted by the Greeks.

'I must mention an occurrence,' he adds towards the end of one of his letters, 'that lately happened to me on crossing a river to draw a cover on the other side.' He is referring to the River Stour, which then and now 'frequently overflows its banks and is also very rapid and dangerous. The flood that morning was, though sudden, extensive; the neighbouring meadows were all laid under water, and only the tops of the hedges appeared. There were posts to direct us to the bridge, but we had a great length of water to pass before we could get at it; it was, besides, so deep that our horses almost swam; and the shortest-legged horses, and longest-legged riders were worst off. The hounds dashed in as usual, and were immediately carried, by the rapidity of the current, a long way down the stream. The huntsman was far behind them; and, as he could advance but slowly, he was constrained to see his hounds wear themselves out in useless contentions with the current, from their efforts to get to him.

'It was a shocking scene! Many of the hounds when they reached the shore had entirely lost the use of their limbs; for it froze, and the cold was intolerable; some lay as if they were dead, and others reeled as if they had been drinking wine. Our ill-luck was not yet complete; the weakest hounds, or such as were most affected by the cold, we now saw entangled in the tops of the hedges, and heard their lamentations. Well known tongues, and such I had never heard before without pleasure. It was painful to see their distress, and not know how to relieve it. A number of people, by this time, were assembled near the riverside; but there was not one amongst them that would venture in. However, a guinea, at last, tempted one man to fetch out a hound that was entangled in a bush, and would otherwise have perished. Two hounds remained upon a hedge all night; and, though at a considerable distance from each other when we left them, yet they got together afterwards; and the next morning, when the flood abated, they were found closely clasping each other; without doubt, it was the friendly warmth which they afforded each other that kept both alive. We lost but one hound, by this unlucky expedition, but could not save any of our terriers. They were seen to sink, their strength not being sufficient to resist the two enemies they had to encounter (powerful when combined): the severity of the cold and the rapidity of the stream.'

Beckford practised what he preached in his books, with accomplishments and linguistic talents that became legendary, as it was said that he would bag a fox in Greek, find a hare in Latin, inspect his kennels in Italian, and direct the management of his stables in exquisite French. Beckford admired Hugo Meynell as the best breeder of hounds, and as another exponent of fox-hunting, but Meynell did not personally hunt hounds.

Peter Beckford was unique as the foremost literary sportsman of his age. His epitaph, in the neat Gothic parish church of Iwerne Stepleton, in parkland grounds beside his house, ignores the power and perpetuity of the printed word: 'We die and are forgotten; tis Heaven's decree. Thus the fate of others will be the fate of me.'

It was in Beckford's time, and in his county and probably with his approval, that the roe deer – a native British species hunted to extinction in the Middle Ages – was released into the woods of central Dorset from Lord Dorchester's park at Milton Abbey. The reintroduction, in 1800, was successful, and roe are now common through southern England, and still enlarging their range. The Roebuck Hounds of Edwin Mansel-Pleydell of Milborne St Andrew, and the New Forest Buckhounds into recent times, would revive their sporting possibilities. For most of their descendants, what passed for culling for nearly two centuries was a succession of unregulated and unsporting shotgun drives, that served to disperse them so effectively that they are now numerically the strongest species of deer in England.

Beckford dedicated his best known book to James John Farquharson, a neighbouring landowner on Cranborne Chase, who will become Dorset's pre-eminent sportsman as our story unfolds.

Peter Beckford, painted in 1779,
from a miniature by John Stuart.

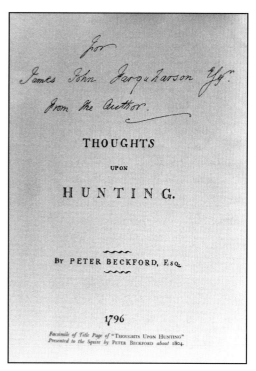

Beckford's title page, on the copy of his
'Thoughts' presented to James John
Farquharson.

Peter Beckford's hounds and hunt servants, in Stepleton Park,
painted by Francis Satorius.

Stepleton House, near Blandford, sketched by Lionel Edwards.

Two couple of Beckford's hounds, featuring Belman, Mannerly,
Belmaid and Guider, painted by Francis Satorius.

Another two couple of Beckford's hounds, painted by Francis Satorius, with Crazy on
the left and Pillager on the right, and Blameless and Brilliant in the middle.

DEATH OF THE FOX,

'Death of the Fox' in a cartoon parody of Beckford's book and times, published in 1812.

Chapter Two

STURT PERIOD

HUMPHRY STURT'S SLASHING RUN

One of the great runs at the turn of the nineteenth century was that with Humphry Sturt's Hounds. Though his ancestral home was Crichel House, near Wimborne, he kept the pack at Clyffe Kennels, beside Clyffe House, on the ridge of gravel and gorse above Tincleton, near Puddletown. The run in question took place in January, either in 1804 or 1805, and would be recalled for the rest of their lives by those veteran sportsmen Robert, James and John Burgess, and John House from Anderson, near Bere Regis.

A stump-tail fox had been dug out at Milton Park and brought over to Clyffe where he was let loose in a cellar. Because of a hard frost he was held for a couple of days before being turned out at Lord's Down, near the old Dewlish Turnpike Gate, at the junction on the Dorchester-Blandford highway with the lane to Crowthorne. He went away over Milborne Farm, jumped fence out of Milborne Eweleaze into the Deer Park, across the open fields and downs for Winterborne Whitechurch, where he turned north-east over Chescombe and Whatcombe Park, and straight ahead over Thornicombe and Down House, crossing the Blandford-Stickland road, down over the wooded Cliff.

Here stump-tail proceeded to swim the icy waters of the River Stour, between Blandford Bridge and the Portman family seat at Bryanston House, and continued eastwards through the Deer Park on to Mill Down. Then he crossed the Higher Blandford Road and went on to Pimperne, skirting the north side of the village, and shot straight on to Tarrant Hinton and Eastbury Park Wall, Chettle village, Thickthorn Farm and Thorney Down. All the time he kept the Blandford-Salisbury turnpike to his right and kept to his chosen north-easterly trajectory. Then he went over Minchington Down and on to Woodyates, beyond Pentridge, where he crossed the earthworks of Bokerley Ditch, and entered Wiltshire at Vernditch Chase.

Straight on he went, by the side of the road, into the big open country that leads to Harnham Hill – overlooking Salisbury – where in olden times the mail-coach horses were changed in stables at the top.

Here, with darkness coming on, stump-tail was lost at the bottom of the steep hill. This wonderfully stout varmint had led the pack for over four hours and a distance of just 30 miles. They never went over the turnpike road but once from start to finish. Those who took part would still be calling it 'the run of the century' for two generations to come. They thought it thoroughly just that not only had 'old stumpy' outrun them, but that he also had the energy and country craft to make his way home again. Three days afterwards the woodsman at Milton Park declared that he was back in the same wood where he was dug out about a week before.

PRINCE GEORGE AND PARSON BILLY BUTLER

George Augustus Frederick, Prince Regent and afterwards George IV (1762-1830; King from 1820) borrowed both Crichel House and its pack of hounds. One of the enduring stories of Dorset hunting through the nineteenth century was that the vicar of Frampton, Rev. William Butler – known familiarly as Billy Butler – became a friend of the Prince after the latter had heard that Billy 'knew the home of every fox in the county'.

The legend was that Mr Butler, having been asked by a royal messenger if he could direct them to a fox, suggested they drew a gorse covert. Pleased with the advice, the Prince trotted off but it proved blank. Mr Butler, however, was not one to sit quietly under defeat. He dismounted and approached the huntsman. 'Which you do your consider your best hound to face a thick place?' the vicar asked. 'I'm sure the fox is at home, but the gorse is so dense the hounds have overdrawn him.'

The huntsman pointed his whip to Trojan and said the old hound was as good as any. To the astonishment of everyone, Billy Butler went up to the dog, stroking him down, and having made friends picked him up in his arms and proceeded to disappear into the gorse bushes. Talking to the hound as he went, he then released him, and induced Trojan to put his nose down. There was a whimper, then he lashed his sides with his stern, and soon he was going full cry through the gorse. The rest of the pack joined in and their fox shot out, to provide a capital run.

The result was friendship between Billy and the Prince, conducted on equal terms, as another anecdote indicates. The Prince invited the hunting incumbent to dinner the following Sunday. 'Well, your Royal Highness, Sunday is a bad day to ask a parson to dine. If your Royal Highness will make it Monday, I will come with pleasure.' Dinner was therefore fixed for Monday.

Billy was also remembered for his terrier, Pompey, which was shaved like a poodle and would be produced when foxes went down a hole. The legendary Billy Butler died in retirement at Okeford Fitzpaine.

Royal hunting in Regency Dorset centred on Humphry Sturt's seat at Crichel House.

Chapter Three

MR FARQUHARSON'S
HOUNDS

MR FARQUHARSON OF LANGTON, EASTBURY AND CATTISTOCK

 On the other side of Blandford from Iwerne Stepleton, at Langton House, in the parish of Langton Long Blandford and from Eastbury House, Tarrant Gunville, James John Farquharson (1785–1871) became Dorset's premier huntsman. Henry Symonds (1817–95) wrote that he 'will always stand foremost' among the staunch patrons of the 'noble science'. His home was at Langton, in parkland beside the River Stour, where he built an elegant oval stable block in Bath stone that was said to be the finest in southern England. Eastbury was provided with kennels for seventy-five couple of hounds and stabling for some fifty horses. He also established a western base, from a hunting-box at Cattistock, and founded its hunting traditions.

Langton carried a welcoming motto above its gate: 'Through this wide opening gate none come too early, none return too late.' On 26 February 1831, when agricultural riots threatened national security, the Home Secretary, Lord Melbourne, confirmed the commission of Mr Farquharson as Captain of Blandford Independent Troop of the Dorset Yeomanry Cavalry. His First Lieutenant was his eldest son, James John Farquharson, Junior, and as Second Lieutenant Henry William Berkeley Portman of Bryanston House. Second son Frederick Thomas Farquharson was Cornet.

For more than half a century (1806–58) Mr Farquharson's Hounds boasted a territory of a thousand square miles, extending in the west from Bridport inland to East Chinnock, Somerset, and in the east from East Chaldon to Blandford and then down the Stour Valley to West Parley. From here the inland frontier swept northwards, beside the Avon Valley, to Verwood, Martin, and the Ox Drove above Broad Chalke. The Wiltshire boundary followed the prehistoric ridgeway around to Ludwell and East Knowle. Its northern line then included Shaftesbury and Gillingham before dropping into the Blackmore Vale from Milton on Stour to Todber and Sturminster Newton. It then projected eastwards to Lydlinch, Bishop's Caundle, Folke,

Lillington, Thornford, Clifton Maybank, and the countryside south of Yeovil. It is quite exhausting just to look at the map.

Their sixty-two meeting places – alphabetically listed and covering four counties – required formidable logistical and travelling arrangements for huntsmen and the field. The season in the west was based at Cattistock rather than Eastbury. The underlying geology has been noted in parenthesis. It was no accident that chalkland venues were disproportionately well represented and this was taken into account, judging by the attendance record of those who relished long distance downland runs.

1. Armswell Farm, near Piddletrenthide, Dorset (chalk)
2. Ashley Wood, near Blandford, Dorset (chalk)
3. Bishop's Caundle, near Lydlinch, Dorset (clay)
4. Boveridge House, near Cranborne, Dorset (chalk)
5. Bradford Peverell, near Dorchester, Dorset (chalk)
6. Buckland Newton, near Cerne Abbas, Dorset (chalk)
7. Buckland Ripers, near Chickerell, Dorset (chalk)
8. Bulbarrow Hill, near Milton Abbas, Dorset (chalk)
9. Chalmington, near Cattistock, Dorset (chalk)
10. Chetnole, near Sherborne, Dorset (clay)
11. Chilcombe, near Bridport, Dorset (chalk)
12. Clifton Wood, near Yetminster, Dorset (clay)
13. Coker Wood, near Yeovil, Somerset (limestone)
14. Compton Valence, near Maiden Newton, Dorset (chalk)
15. Crichel House, near Wimborne, Dorset (chalk)
16. Deadmoor Common, near Fifehead Neville (clay)
17. Dewlish House, near Dorchester, Dorset (chalk)
18. Dole's Ash, near Piddletrenthide, Dorset (chalk)
19. Druce Farm, near Puddletown, Dorset (chalk)
20. Duncliffe Wood, near Shaftesbury, Dorset (clay)
21. East Knowle, near Hindon, Wiltshire (greensand)
22. Ferne House, near Ludwell, Wiltshire (greensand)
23. Forston, near Charminster, Dorset (chalk)
24. Gaunt's House, near Wimborne, Dorset (sand)
25. Glanvilles Wootton, near Sherborne, Dorset (clay)
26. Godmanstone, near Cerne Abbas, Dorset (chalk)
27. Handley Common, near Sixpenny Handley, Dorset (chalk)
28. Harley Wood, near Gussage All Saints, Dorset (chalk)

29. High Hall, near Wimborne, Dorset (chalk)

30. Holcombe Bottom, near Piddlehinton, Dorset (chalk)

31. Honeycomb Wood, near Sherborne, Dorset (limestone)

32. King Grove, near Piddletrenthide, Dorset (chalk)

33. Kingsettle, near Donhead St Andrew, Wiltshire (greensand)

34. Kingston Lacy House, near Wimborne, Dorset (chalk)

35. Kingston Russell House, near Bridport, Dorset (chalk)

36. Knighton, near Broad Chalke, Wiltshire (chalk)

37. Longburton, near Sherborne, Dorset (clay)

38. Long Crichel, near Wimborne, Dorset (chalk)

39. Martin Wood, near Fordingbridge, Hampshire (chalk)

40. Melcombe Park, near Milton Abbas, Dorset (chalk)

41. Milton Abbas, near Blandford, Dorset (chalk)

42. Moreton House, near Wool, Dorset (sand)

43. North Perrott Manor, near Crewkerne, Somerset (limestone)

44. Pen Wood, near Yeovil, Somerset (limestone)

45. Piddles Wood, near Sturminster Newton, Dorset (clay)

46. Puncknowle Manor, near Bridport, Dorset (clay)

47. Rampisham, near Maiden Newton, Dorset (chalk)

48. Revels Inn, near Cerne Abbas, Dorset (chalk)

49. Short Wood, near Mappowder, Dorset (clay)

50. Spetisbury Down, near Blandford, Dorset (chalk)

51. Sydling Barn, near Sydling St Nicholas, Dorset (chalk)

52. Turnworth House, near Blandford, Dorset (chalk)

53. Uddens House, near Wimborne, Dorset (sand)

54. Up Cerne House, near Cerne Abbas, Dorset (chalk)

55. Warmwell House, near Dorchester, Dorset (sand)

56. Whitfield Woods, near Yetminster, Dorset (clay)

57. Winterbourne Steepleton, near Dorchester, Dorset (chalk)

58. Winyard's Gap, near Maiden Newton, Dorset (chalk)

59. Woodcutts Common, near Sixpenny Handley, Dorset (chalk)

60. Wynford House, near Maiden Newton, Dorset (chalk)

61. Wytherstone, near Powerstock, Dorset (clay)

62. Yellowham Wood, near Puddletown, Dorchester (sand)

Throughout his half century, the Squire of Langton 'had the good fortune to command in his two huntsmen the services of Ben Jennings and James ('Jem') Treadwell, both consummate masters of the craft.' Solomon Baker was the whipper-in.

TWENTY MILES, FROM MELCOMBE TO YETMINSTER

Though a good third short of Humphry Sturt's record run, one of the best runs for Mr Farquharson's Hounds took place in 1820, when their fox ran downhill from Melcombe Park to Short Wood, Beaulieu, Castle Hill, Glanvilles Wootton. From here he went across the Blackmore Vale to Holnest, passing between Grange Woods and Butterwick, on to Holme Bushes, Leweston House, Whitfield Wood and into the stone quarries at Yetminster.

There, after a good twenty miles, Charlie slipped under the big rocks and saved his brush for another day.

RUNNING FOX AND HORSES TO GROUND IN DORCHESTER

It was towards the end of 1822 that Mr Farquharson's Hounds had an extraordinarily clipping run. Henry Symonds wrongly remembered the year as 1825 but earlier accounts exist. Meeting at Buckland Ripers, north of Chickerell, they found a fox and broke away over to Dairyhouse Coppice, and Culver Willow Bed, and slowly via Waddon and Corton to where the Hardy Monument now stands. In this long heather on Black Down they may have transferred to a fresh fox out of a gravel pit.

It was a runner, down over the Dorchester-Abbotsbury Road, to Bridehead and the Gorwell covers, over the hill to Lower Kingston Russell, crossing the meadows and going up the steep hill into the big downs. Having crossed the Dorchester-Bridport road he put his head straight over Higher Kingston Russell Farm and then went over the Roman Road into East Compton Farm. The next section of the chase was over Southover Farm and Littlewood Farm into Frampton Court.

He then went down through the water-meadows of the River Frome to Grimstone, Stratton and Bradford Peverell. From this place the horses began to stand still – one after the other – and the lance was freely used. The chase resumed over Fordington Down to Poundbury, thence to Dorchester Barracks and the Top o' Town. Our stout fox ran down Durngate Street, into the Plume of Feathers yard and into a closet.

He was brought out and killed. So great was the excitement in the County Town that the judges closed the Assize Courts and came out to see the fun. Lots of the horses died in Fordington Fields and in the town that night. Many more were of little use afterwards. Yet horses at that time of year were in good hunting trim.

Mr House takes the brush at Upwey, after eight miles in 40 minutes

Farmer Sansom, the Duke of Bedford's tenant at Kingston Russell, made sure there was a good fox in the appropriately named Foxholes withybed when Mr Farquharson's Hounds met on the downs west of Dorchester on 14 December 1827. Romulus and Gertrude led the music with a crash of canine vocality as a choker of a struggle began with their gallant prey making off for the woods of Littlebredy and the cow-leaze of Winterbourne Steepleton before turning south for Black Down, or Blagdon as it was called, and followed the Ridgeway eastwards to pass above Martinstown and Ashton.

Then he dropped down into the fields around Upwey and was pulled down in the open after eight miles in 40 minutes without a single check. A large field started but few were placed at the end to see the patriarchal and benevolent smile of the Squire of Langton cheering his noble pack. Mr Farquharson's two sons were also up-front with the huntsman Ben Jennings and the chosen few, to see the brush fairly won by seventeen-year-old Mr House from Anderson, near Bere Regis.

Twenty-four miles around the Piddle and Cerne valleys

Another marvellous day's sport for Mr Farquharson's Hounds took place on 13 November 1835. This was a meet in Yellowham Wood, beside the Dorchester-Puddletown turnpike, and Ben Jennings took the hounds into the south-west corner. They soon found and broke away for Chine Hill and Waterston Farm, from where their fox then turned south up and over Ridge Way, to skirt the western side of Grey's Wood.

From here he headed north-west, running along Waterston Ridge, westwards to Wolfeton Clump. Then he went north again to Piddlehinton Down and Four Mile Hill (named for its milestone), over the Old Sherborne Road, and south-west along the spur of downland in a line for Mr Goodenough's on Cowdon Hill at Godmanstone.

Here he turned north once more, up the eastern side of the Cerne Valley, for King Grove and Nether Cerne. Next he passed Mr Hart's dairy-house and then turned westwards, across the water-meadows and the Dorchester-Cerne turnpike, heading uphill in the direction of Sydling St Nicholas.

Here he was turned by a party of rabbit shooters and went to earth at Holcombe. It had been a run of 55 minutes, over ten miles, and was mutually agreed to have been as good a run as had been seen for some years.

The hounds were then taken to Mr Goodenough's gorse, at Cowdon, and went away up the opposite side of the hill with their heads up and sterns down, close up. Across the enclosures he went, for two miles over Godmanstone Down, and then turned southwards for Grimstone. Suddenly he altered his mind, turning west to take off over the Sydling Water and its meadows, up the hill, and into Frampton Plantation.

He was headed at the far end and turned short, back and down the hill to Magiston, where he re-crossed the Sydling water-meadows. Moving on to Godmanstone South Down, he turned north for Sydling Down and then east, to skirt Cerne Park. Straight on he went, north to the Admiralty Telegraph Station and High Stoy. Then he turned west and sunk into the Blackmore Vale for a circuit of Hilfield, then up the hill to Hanover, after which the pace began to tell. 'Bellows to mend,' was the general cry, with some trotting, others walking, and the rest at a standstill.

The fox went from here to the south-west, limping across Batcombe Hill, and into Sydling Barn Wood, where a fresh varmint was holloaed. Ben Jennings stopped the hounds. It had been an incredible second run of 145 minutes, with hardly a check in what must have reached 14 miles, and but for the unfortunate holloa he would have been killed there, at about two-and-a-half hours. Thus ended as good a day as anyone had seen. Though Ben appeared to be getting younger, the day had taken its toll on the horses, several of which could not reach home. The veterinary surgeons were much in request but there was no news of any casualties.

Ten miles in 100 minutes, from Deadmoor to Duncliffe

Mr Farquharson's Hounds met at Deadmoor Common, Fifehead Neville, on 26 January 1836, to pay their respects to an old fox who had led them many miles on former occasions. Ben Jennings took them away, in firm and melodious voice, to Puxey Common and the enclosures of Bagber and the River Stour at the top of their speed.

Reynard crossed the river, as usual making his way for Marnhull, where interspersed roads and fallow fields brought them to a long check. Then Ben's superior head soon put them right again and they crossed the upper river for Fifehead Magdalen. This old varmint was lost after a run of ten miles, without a turn, in 100 minutes.

No doubt he is the same fox which was killed at Duncliffe Hill, by Mr Portman's Hounds, on 15 February 1836.

DINNER AT THE KING'S ARMS FOLLOWED BY A FOX AT PULHAM

The 1836 hunt dinner for the followers of Mr Farquharson's Hounds, at the King's Arms in Dorchester on 5 March, had its sequel next morning with 200 horsemen out, for a meet at King Grove, near Piddletrenthide. They found a fox, and went away with a good scent, north-westwards to the Old Sherborne Road and Giant's Head. From here he headed to Holcombe, Hawcombe, Eight Acre Coppice and sank into the Blackmore Vale via Clinger Farm and between Revels Inn and Castle Hill, down over Duntish Common to Pulham Farm. They killed him there, in Mr Bullen's pigsty, without a check.

Tatchel Bullen had three awful falls, from a horse which had been lent to him for the day, but was not much hurt.

WHO-WHOOPING OVER THE GORWELL FOX AND REV. BILLY BUTLER

On 14 November 1838, Mr Farquharson's Hounds were invited to Gorwell Farm, between Abbotsbury and Littlebredy, where Henry Symonds' father wanted them to kill a fox which had been raiding his poultry. It had been Jem Treadwell's first season with Mr Farquharson, after he left Henry Hall and the Blackmore Vale, having arrived at Eastbury Kennels in 1837. Henry Symonds remembered hearing Rev. William Butler telling his mother, with her five children in the dining-room, to 'look at the olive branches about thy table'.

They found their fat old customer in Broad Coppice and went over through Hanging Coppice and Park Coppice, and over the ups and downs to Bridehead Farm. From here they ascended the steep hill to Steepleton Down and he then headed north to Winterbourne Plantation and west over the open downs to Kingston Russell, where the hounds caught him jumping a wall. Billy Butler fell off his horse and a visiting Frenchman was taken to task for saying 'what a pity he did not die'. The man explained his thinking: 'We could cry de Who-Whoop over de fox and de Billy Butler at de same time!'

Mr Farquharson recalled that he had invited the Frenchman to dinner with the suggestion that he should change his shirt. 'No thank you,' he said, 'I shirted yesterday.'

JEM TREADWELL LOSES HIS MOUNT AT UPWEY

Mr Farquharson's Hounds met at Buckland Wood, Buckland Ripers, on 23 November 1838 and found a fox which headed from Chickerell into the Weymouth hinterland, in the direction of Nottington and Broadway. It then turned north, up the Upwey valley and brook, which was a little uphill, with a high fence on the take-off side.

Jem Treadwell's young horse failed to clear the wide, deep ditch on the other side, dislocating both points at the shoulder. Harry Nash, the eminent veterinary surgeon, told Mr Farquharson that nothing could be done but shoot it. The horse was bought only the week before for 120 guineas.

Treadwell transferred to one of the whip's horses and went on after the hounds, northwards across the hills to Bronkham, where he got up to the pack at the first check, and on Reynard's line again, westwards across Martinstown and Steepleton fields, to run into him at Winterbourne Abbas, near the Coach and Horses Inn.

Jem Treadwell, who was then 38-years-old, would remember it as the one and only day when his master was very angry with him. 'You must be more careful how you ride a young horse at a blind fence,' he was told.

A REMARKABLE SCENT FROM BLAGDON LEAVES SCOTS GREYS AT A STANDSTILL

Another Buckland Wood meet, at Buckland Ripers on 6 December 1838, found their fox in Clover Coppice at Shilvinghampton and followed it across the vale to the steep hill where the Hardy Monument now stands. It had gone over Blagdon to Steepleton Eweleazes, and through Winterbourne Plantation, over the Dorchester-Bridport turnpike, to Kingston Russell Farm and East Compton. Here several of the horses, belonging to officers of the Scots Greys who were then stationed at Dorchester, stood still.

The whip, Penny, could not go any further. Those who did struggle on saw the hounds earth their fox at Winholes Coppice, West Compton, above Wynford Eagle. This was a most trying and brilliant run, of some 12 miles.

SOME 'HARE' DOING TEN MILES, VIA THE CHESIL BEACH

Meeting at Kingston Russell on 23 December 1838, Mr Farquharson's Hounds had a bad beginning with a ringing fox, which was quickly killed, providing little sport. Next day they were going to Eastbury Park for Christmas, and were not due back at Cattistock until February, so the large field was hoping for another fox. It was two o'clock when Mr Sampson said there was a fox in the willow-bed near the dairy-house.

Off it went, southwards over the hill and through the Gorwell and Ashley Chase covers, to

Puncknowle Wood and East Bexington. It then followed the Chesil Beach to Abbotsbury Castle (the seaside mansion of the Ilchester family, rather than the hill-fort), with hares scattering in all directions. Jem Treadwell had to check them here, and Harry Templer, from Bridport, told him: 'I think you are on a hare.'

Treadwell reacted angrily: 'What the (expletive) do you think Mr Farquharson keeps servants for, but to know if they are hunting a fox or a hare?'

Then he blew his horn, saw two or three leading hounds on Reynard's line, and crossed the road into the Decoy (Abbotsbury Swannery), all through the spear beds (reeds), where he turned inland for a mile to Elworth and went on through Wyke Wood to the Fleet in another mile. Having bore on to the plantations of Langton Herring, and crossed the Abbotsbury-Weymouth road, the moon was shining brightly and the hounds running for blood in a further mile. Treadwell told Henry Symonds to ride on to see if the fox reached Buckland Wood.

He saw him fail a field short of the wood. The fox no longer had the strength to clear a low wall and lay down before the hounds, 'as good a fox as ever ran'. Horses all tired, after a first-class ten miles, and everyone feeling a long way from the kennels and home.

Down the Frome Valley, from West Stafford to Wool

Mr Farquharson's Hounds visited South Dorset, from Eastbury, on 22 January 1839 and stayed overnight at Mr Groves' at West Knighton. The next day they met at West Stafford, courtesy John Floyer M.P. of Stafford House, and found in Friarmayne willow-bed, at Broadmayne. Over the meadows he went, to Knighton Plantation, Warmwell sheep-wash, and Warmwell Wood. Then he turned across the enclosures to Hope Wood and Galton Common, down by the side of the long bog to Tadnoll Mill.

He resumed his eastwards line down the Frome Valley by crossing Winfrith Heath and Burton Common Heath, leaving Moreton Obelisk on Fir Hill to the north, and then crossed the river to Bovington. Here, with his strength failing after a demanding eight miles, he ran a few small covers downstream to the Elizabethan mansion at Woolbridge Manor, where he was killed in a cow-shed.

Frederick Farquharson was with the field that day and went on to a hunt ball at Handsford Inn for the night. Others went over to John Porter's at Clyffe House, Tincleton, to give the horses and themselves a rest. Old Ben Jennings had pointed Jem Treadwell through the difficult country.

EDWARD POPE WINS THE SCUFFLE FOR A BRUSH AT CHILCOMBE

Having returned to Cattistock from their mid-winter break at Eastbury, Mr Farquharson's Hounds met at Kingcombe Coppice, above Toller Porcorum, on 6 February 1839. They found and went away to Hooke Park, Wytherstone, Powerstock Common, Barrowland, on to Wynford Big Wood, West Compton, and over the Roman Road for Kingston Russell.

Here he turned westwards, over Long Bredy and Litton Down to Stancombe, and then turned south over Askerswell Down to cross the Dorchester-Bridport turnpike and on to Chilcombe. Here he entered Coombe Coppice and was killed on the down close by. Eliza Hutchings of Broadwindsor, and Edward Pope of Toller, had a fair scuffle about the brush; Mr Farquharson decided that Mr Pope should have the coveted prize.

FAST-MOVING TWELVE MILES, FROM PUNCKNOWLE TO RIDGEWAY HILL

Having met at Puncknowle Wood on 20 February 1839, Mr Farquharson's Hounds moved off towards the coast at East Bexington and turned to the east to run over Wears Hill, Abbotsbury, to Broad Coppice, Gorwell. The fox then went on to Bridehead and over the hill to Blagdon, where the Hardy Monument now stands, and continued south-east over Bronkham Hill to Friar Waddon.

On he went, north-westwards by Ashton hamlet and Winterborne Monkton, and then south to the Upwey quarries, where they rolled him over in the Dorchester-Weymouth turnpike road, where the tunnel now is on Ridgeway Hill. It had been a fast-moving twelve miles.

SPLENDID RUN, FROM DUDDLE HEATH, TO THE SHITTERTON EARTH

Operating from Cattistock on 8 November 1839, Mr Farquharson's Hounds met at Yellowham Wood, beside the Dorchester-Puddletown turnpike, and found a mile to the south, on Duddle Heath. Their fox ran across Ilsington Heath and through Ilsington Wood, over to Tincleton Hangings, then eastwards over Mr Crane's land at Southover Heath.

Leaving Sares Wood and the gravel ridge to the south he then dropped into the water-meadows of the River Piddle and followed these downstream beside the hamlets of Briantspuddle, Throop and Turners Puddle.

Here he turned, via Spring Gardens, and then went up and over Black Hill, to descend into the next valley and cross the Bere Stream in the hamlet of Shitterton, at Bere Regis. Then he headed west, up the slope, and went into the main earth at the end of Piddle Wood, opposite Roke Brakes. It had been a splendid run of eight miles without a check.

ELEVEN MILES, FROM WEST COMPTON TO BRIDPORT HARBOUR

Mr Farquharson's Hounds met at Compton Barn, West Compton, on 13 November 1839, and found in Winholes Coppice. They went straight away to Wynford Big Coppice and on to Barrowland, Wytherstone, then across Powerstock Common and over Eggardon Hill.

On the south side he sunk into the vale, to Askerswell, and went on to the Travellers' Rest, where he crossed the Bridport-Dorchester turnpike. He made first for Shipton Gorge and then headed seawards, along North Hill above Burton Bradstock, to Wych Farm on the slope overlooking West Bay. This was now his final mile and he lay down in a ditch close to Bridport Harbour to give the hounds their richly deserved prize. It had been an eleven-mile run.

DARKNESS WINS AFTER FOURTEEN MILES, FROM CHILCOMBE TO MAGISTON

A bad morning was had by Mr Farquharson's Hounds on 24 November 1839 – around Chilcombe and Little Berwick – after meeting at the Travellers' Rest, on the turnpike east of Bridport. They then found about two o'clock in Hodder's Coppice. This mangy stump-tail went off eastwards over Litton Cheney water-meadows and then embarked on a southern loop through Look Wood, Chapel Coppice, and Ashley Covers, into a northward curve to Long Bredy and over the hills. These included Kingston Russell and East Compton, and two miles of the Roman Road, on to Frampton Hogleazes.

By now, after twelve miles, all the horses had had enough. Treadwell still held the hounds on his line through Frampton Park and for a further couple of miles over the Maiden Newton road and the Dorchester-Yeovil turnpike, into the Sydling valley. Here, with darkness coming on, they had to give up at Magiston. 'Never mind, Jem,' an old sportsman from Tarrant Launceston consoled him. 'It's a very pretty pastime.'

TWELVE MILES, OVER TRYING COUNTRY, AND THE VIRTUES OF 'MURPHY'

Having met at Wynford Eagle and found in Wynford Big Wood, on 4 December 1839, Mr Farquharson's Hounds went away westwards to Barrowland and Wytherstone. Then they headed north to Hooke Park and turned back to Powerstock and Brown's Farm. Next they were crossing the vale to Askerswell, Nallers Farm, and Stancombe. Then over the hill to

Litton Down, where the hounds had killed their fox after twelve miles and eaten all but the head, when Jem Treadwell got to them.

He was riding the grey portrayed in Mr Farquharson's presentation picture. 'Paddy from Cork', or 'Murphy' as he was otherwise known, was the best horse for a trying run that anyone had seen. Several horses were so beaten that they could not get over the steep hill by Coombe Gate and had to be left for the night at Askerswell and in Stancombe Barn.

SHERIDAN ASIDE TO TWELVE-MILE RUN FROM BRADFORD PEVERELL TO PUNCKNOWLE

Having returned again to Cattistock from Eastbury Kennels, Mr Farquharson's Hounds met at Bradford Plantation, south of Bradford Peverell, on 25 November 1840. They found in the large furze brake and went away north-west over Skippet Farm and Littlewood Farm. The large field then crossed Hogleazes, which were familiar to older followers for the numerous coursing meetings which used to be held there each year, courtesy of Lieutenant-General Sir Colquhoun Grant of Frampton Court before Richard Brinsley Sheridan – the son of the statesman and dramatist of the same name – married his heiress, Marcia Maria Grant.

From Great Hogleaze the fox turned south-west, crossing the Roman Road, and then the Dorchester-Bridport turnpike, at Kingston Russell. Next were the downs to Long Bredy and then the water-meadows at Litton Cheney. Then there was a sharp turn to the south, for Goole and Puncknowle Wood, where this old customer went into the main earth. It had been a long run, of twelve miles, ending far from home for most of the field.

THREE HOURS FROM MELCOMBE PARK TO BERE WOOD AND MILBORNE WOOD

Mr Farquharson's Hounds met at Melcombe Barn on 11 December 1840 and found in Melcombe Park. After 90 minutes in cover, a fox left for Breach Wood, leaving Ansty Brewery to the south, and headed south-east through Higher Ansty to the Hilton Plantations. It then turned south, across Cheselbourne Common and Dewlish Common, to Coles Hill Barn, above Milborne St Andrew. From here it went straight through Milborne Wood and crossed the Dorchester-Blandford turnpike.

Leaving Milborne Field Barn (West End Barn) to the west it continued southwards to Tolpuddle Common and then turned east, crossing the water-meadows at Roger's Hill, to Roke Farm, Bere Down, and Muddox Barrow. Sanctuary was now on the horizon, in the wilds of Bere Wood, but the fox was headed and turned short to the north-west, leaving Winterborne Kingston parish to the east.

On went the fox, through Saint Loe's Coppice and across the London Road at Winterborne Whitechurch, through Chescombe Farm to Cayles Down Copse. It was now heading south-east and having crossed the Milton Abbas road, between Bagber Farm and Hewish Farm, it made straight for Milborne Wood. The run had now reached 120 minutes and covered 13 miles, with the going very heavy and wet, and only one horse still able to canter. This was a fine chestnut, purchased by Mr Graham of Weymouth from George Richards of High Chaldon Farm, Winfrith.

The hounds were also almost beat and it took them another 60 minutes, at dusk, to kill their five-year-old dog fox in a ditch near Milborne Fair-ground. Jem Treadwell said it was the hardest run since he carried a horn. Eighty horsemen had been reduced to a score who were there at the end to hear the who-whoop. There would be a further endurance of 18 miles to return to kennels.

ANOTHER THIRTEEN MILES, FROM MILBORNE WOOD TO FRAMPTON PARK

The next time Mr Farquharson's Hounds visited Milborne Wood was for the meet there on 9 January 1841. They found and went away westwards to Dewlish House, Bason Hill, Druce Farm and Burn Coppice. From here, crossing the Piddlehinton road at Muston, the fox went on to Waterston Ridge, Wolfeton Clump and through Lord Ilchester's brake to Forston. Having crossed the Cerne Abbas turnpike, it continued westwards to Stratton Down and Grimstone Down.

Then it sunk into the Frome valley, as if for Maiden Newton Coppice, but turned south through Hyde Plantation, over the River Frome into Frampton Park, and was lost at Littlewood. Samuel Davis lived there at the time. It had been a long and severe run, of 13 miles, and the general assumption was that the fox must have died.

A TEN-MILE RUN FROM MILBORNE WOOD TO DUNTISH

Mr Farquharson's Hounds were back in Milborne Wood on 1 November 1841. They soon found a fox they had hunted twice before, over the same line, and followed a good scent over the Dewlish road to Bagber Coppice and Cheselbourne Fields, to Bingham's Melcombe, then over Hilton Down to Ansty Brewery (now the Village Hall and Fox Inn).

Here the hounds had lost in the previous seasons, but this time he still had them close to him, as he went on to Breach Wood, through Melcombe Park, and on without a turn to Alton Common. He then took to the Blackmore Vale, for Beaulieu, leaving Buckland Knoll on the left. They pulled him down in the shrubbery under Castle Hill House at Duntish. It had been a grand run of ten miles.

ELEVEN MILES, FROM UDDENS TO THICKTHORN DOWN

Mr Farquharson's Hounds met at Uddens House on 29 January 1842 and went away across Holt Heath, north-westwards to Chalbury Hill. He continued westwards, through Crichel Park, and then the entirety of the huge Chetterwood. On he went to a brilliant finish, northwards over the hills, and from scent to view. Here he was killed, on Thickthorn Down, after eleven miles without a check.

SIXTEEN MILES OF PLOUGH AND DOWN, FROM KINGSTON LACY TO PENTRIDGE

Meeting at the Decoy Pond, Kingston Lacy, on 30 January 1842, Mr Farquharson's Hounds went off after a scent to Badbury Rings. Then they continued northwards from the Bankes Estate into the Crichel Estate and worked the plantations and covers of Chetterwood. The downs by Long Crichel took them into the Shaftesbury Estate, through Oakley Wood, and onwards past Woodyates Inn. Here their fox left the level ground beside the turnpike and headed for Pentridge Hill.

Mr Farquharson, on old Champion, was among the few to see Jem Treadwell get off Poplin and give the who-whoop. Poplin was an Irish mare, as was Murphy, the grey, who carried Treadwell on so many good runs and did the celebrated 14-feet drop in Buckland country. It had been an outstanding run of 16 miles across plough and down.

SWIFT SEVEN MILES, FROM MILBORNE WOOD TO KINGROVE

Mr Farquharson's Hounds were back in Milborne Wood on 17 November 1842. The clinkers soon found and went away to the west, over Chebbard Farm and Dole's Hill, then down into Piddlehinton where he crossed the road as if making for Forston and Nether Cerne.

On the downs, however, he made a northwards turn beside the former turnpike that has become the Old Sherborne Road. His final mile was along the Piddletrenthide side of the ridgeway, to College Down and Little Kingrove. Here he crossed two fields and was killed jumping the hedge into Big Kingrove. It had been a swift chase, with just the one turn, across seven miles of open downland.

Six stiff miles, from Deadmoor Common to Revels Inn

Meeting in the heart of the Blackmore Vale, at Fifehead Neville, on 4 January 1843, Mr Farquharson's Hounds found in Deadmoor Common. They set off westwards through Rooksmoor and Hazelbury Common to the Green Man at King's Stag and then south to the church at Pulham. The fox then turned again, northwards into the stiff country to Holwell Plantation, and curved westwards then south in a loop through Glanvilles Wootton that left Castle Hill to the east.

The hounds closed on him through Black Allers and across the open country between Chandler's Coppice and Woodfalls. This was the final mile and they ran into him in full view under Eight Acre Coppice, behind Revels Inn, near Dogbury Gate. That day Henry Symonds, our principal informant, was on Jack Tar – a black horse – and right well he was carried. It had only been six miles but the vale makes for tough riding.

Revels Inn, at the foot of the downs near Middlemarsh, was used in coaching days for changing horses when the Old Sherborne Road was turnpiked, before the new Cerne Valley turnpike was made from Dorchester to Sherborne. Ben Jennings used to pay his earth-stoppers from Cattistock country at Revels Inn and they would keep it up right merrily for three days. On the other side of the county, operating from Eastbury, he paid his men at Horton Inn.

From Armswell to a 'treeing', at Kingston Maurward

Mr Farquharson's Hounds met on 2 March 1843 in the delightful countryside below the Dorsetshire Gap, at Armswell Farm, and went away at once across the middle ground to Bookham Farm and Buckland Knoll. They then crossed the road between Alton Pancras and Buckland Newton and turned southwards and upwards, on to the high downs above Cerne Abbas, crossing Giant's Head and running on the Piddletrenthide side of the former turnpike to Kingrove.

Here he turned south-west, towards Nether Cerne, and crossed Forston Farm to Lord Ilchester's brake and veered south-eastwards to Wolfeton Clump and Burton Farm, continuing over the top-lands of Charminster parish, where the school now stands. He turned through Henry Mayo's farm and being nearly beat, lay down in a large piece of turnips and rape.

This long check roused the populace of Dorchester who flocked out, hearing the hounds, like Bedlam let loose. Jem Treadwell knew the fox was there and kept on casting. After a bit, someone saw Reynard laying out straight in the middle of the turnip field. They whipped him up, crossed two fields, and killed him under a huge tree in Stinsford Park, beside Kingston Maurward House.

James Penny, the whip, climbed the tree and held the fox over the hounds, for the Dorchester folks to witness what 'treeing' a fox means. They bayed and jostled to dislodge the vanquished prey. It had been an enjoyable twelve miles, with a memorable ending, both for the field and the town.

From Bradford Peverell to the Asylum and Higher Waterston

Mr Farquharson's Hounds met at Martinstown on 16 March 1843 and drew the furze-brakes on Hawkin's Farm. These were blank and they headed north for a mile into the Bradford Plantations on the other side of the Dorchester-Bridport turnpike. From here they were away at once, northwards across the large arable and eweleazes, and had soon crossed the River Frome water-meadows by Stratton village. Straight ahead they went, over Stratton Downs, and then eastwards down and over the Cerne-Dorchester turnpike, and on where the new Asylum now stands (County Mental Hospital, later Herrison Hospital, which replaced the 1832-built Forston Asylum and was opened in 1864).

Then he crossed the former turnpike, the Old Sherborne Road, to Lord Ilchester's house, and was heading south-east, across the downs to Wolfeton Clump. He was leaving a breast-high scent as he went southwards down to Coker's Frome Farm. From here he headed back north and then went east, along Waterston Ridge – as if for Grey's Wood and Yellowham – but altered his mind. Being so hard-pressed he then turned north, over Higher Waterston Farm, and went to ground in a deep pit in a hedgerow where many a litter of cubs have been bred, close to James Harding's house and the kennels of his Mountain Harriers. He had led the pack some eight miles and disappeared with only moments to spare.

George Whieldon falls and others balk at the Butterwick fence

Meeting at Short Wood, near Mappowder, on 3 November 1843, with the usual large field that gathers the day after the Sturminster Newton Show, Mr Farquharson's Hounds drew it blank. They moved westwards to the little Beaulieu spinney and were off like a shot with Reynard and the pack over the little River Lydden and on across the stiff enclosures and road from Buckland Newton to Pulham, to Duntish Common.

Here John Floyer M.P., of Stafford House, and Henry Symonds from Milborne St Andrew on his chestnut, had the field to themselves, having made a good start over the brook. Treadwell and Penny then joined them and they went on to the big earths on Dungeon Hill and Castle Hill, above Duntish Elms. These were closed. So he crossed the road into Black Allers and the Glanvilles Wootton covers, making as if for Grange Woods at Middlemarsh. Then, turning north, he went straight for Butterwick Wood.

This was notorious for a big double fence with a drop on the other side. Jem Treadwell knew it well and yelled to Henry Symonds to jump it as fast as he could. Treadwell carried it off with a fine leap, on The Prince, which was his favourite horse for the Blackmore Vale. As they reached Butterwick the fox disappeared. 'Butterwick Jack', the old hands muttered.

So ended a quick run, in six miles, but a number had bad falls. George Whieldon, who would afterwards be Master of the Vine Hounds, had the hind foot of his horse strike his forehead and scalp him. Frederick House of Anderson Manor, riding Dainty, came to the rescue and tied his handkerchief around his head. He would receive a silver cigar case for his kindness.

UNCHECKED SEVEN MILES FROM WHITFIELD WOODS TO MUDFORD BRIDGE

Another big Blackmore Vale meet of Mr Farquharson's Hounds, attracting 200 horsemen, took place at Whitfield Woods, Lillington, on 7 March 1844. They found in a moment and the fox broke in full view of the large field. There was a good scent which had everyone surging towards a rotten brook. Soon there were quite 20 horses and men foundering about in it.

Meanwhile, across and ahead, Henry Symonds and Frederick House were over a mile away and approaching Honeycomb Wood, having left Leweston House to the east. Then Mr House had a bad fall over a double hedge, and would not be seen again that day. Leaving chaos behind him, the varmint went straight on, northwards across the racecourse on Lenthay Common, Sherborne, and continued into Somerset where he was lost near Mudford Bridge, without a check. He had bounded across eight miles, though this was little compared with Henry Symonds' endurance. Having ridden 20 miles to the meet, from Milborne St Andrew, he would cover more than 50 miles before he was home that night.

AFTER THE WEDDING, ELEVEN MILES FROM MAPPOWDER TO MELBURY PARK

Having been married the previous day, Henry Symonds was accompanied by his brother-in-law, Robert Fookes, from Weston, near Bath, for the meet of Mr Farquharson's Hounds on 27 November 1844. Fashionably dressed in white cord trousers, Robert was mounted on Henry's chestnut horse, for the ride to the meet at Short Wood, near Mappowder, deep in the Blackmore Vale.

They were soon away to Beaulieu Wood, over the River Lydden, on to Duntish Common, and past Castle Hill. Then they crossed the road and covered the stiff section of the vale south-westwards towards Revels Inn, leaving Chandlers Coppice and Woodfalls to the south.

From here they crossed the Cerne-Sherborne turnpike near the White Horse at Middlemarsh and went right through Grange Woods, on a northerly course to Totnell Corner, then turning south-west through Hilfield and Batcombe. Having passed Mr Cockeram's plantation they went on to the Dorchester-Yeovil turnpike at Holywell. On the other side, in Melbury Park, the pack pulled him down in fine style after a grand run of eleven miles.

TRYING PACE FROM CHESELBOURNE COMMON TO ALTON PANCRAS

Having met at Dewlish House on 8 January 1845, and drawn Milborne Wood and the other covers uncharacteristically blank, Mr Farquharson was approached at two o'clock by Henry Symonds with the suggestion that they should go elsewhere: 'Will you go and draw Lord Rivers' new brake on Cheselbourne Common? It has never been drawn.'

'Go on, Treadwell,' he said. 'See what sort of a place it is.'

No sooner had they arrived than out went a brace of foxes. The pack were away with one, north-westwards across the valley and over the road, leaving Bingham's Melcombe to the north. They went over Henning Hill and sunk the hill, over the road from Cheselbourne to Ansty, on to Mr Davis' cottages on the hill.

The pace and the scent were so strong that some of the horses stood still. The hounds were across Lyscombe Bottom, below the hillside covers, and went on westwards over Higher Hill, down to Plush and straight ahead up the next slope, to kill in front of Alton House at Alton Pancras. It had only been five miles but at a most trying pace. Edward Pope, from Toller Porcorum, accompanied Henry Symonds back to Milborne St Andrew that night, and slept. He was on a capital grey and Symonds was on Black Tar. Both horses had been bought from Longman's Green Man Stables in Dorchester.

FAST EIGHT MILES, FROM TOLPUDDLE COMMON TO CHESELBOURNE

The Valentine's Day meet of Mr Farquharson's Hounds, on 14 February 1845, was at Druce. They wasted the morning with a ringing fox which followed the hedgerows beside the River Piddle upstream to Waterston where it was killed.

Returning via Tolpuddle Common, they drew what little furze that was then growing there, and found. This fox was up to a run and crossed Mr James Brine's pair of farms at Tolpuddle and passed through Admiston en route for the Athelhampton water-meadows which stretch north along the Devil's Brook to Fryer's Bridge and the Blandford turnpike on Bason Hill. They went through both Bason Plantation and Warren Plantation, then going over the Puddletown to Cheselbourne road and across the expanse of Druce Down, to veer westwards over Chebbard Farm towards Dole's Hill.

Then he turned north-east, to the Manor Farm home of James Caines at Cheselbourne, and was killed in the orchard in front of the house. It had been a fast eight miles.

FOX AND A HORSE DROP TOGETHER AT STOKE WAKE

A large field gathered to meet Mr Farquharson's Hounds at Short Wood, Mappowder, on 28 February 1845. They soon found and were away to Humber Wood and away northwards over the brook towards Pulham, and then the Green Man Inn at King's Stag. Then he turned east, across Hazelbury Common and Deadmoor Common, and carried on to Fifehead Neville.

Here he turned south, to follow the stream to Locketts Farm, and left Hazelbury Bryan to the west as he tried to get over the chalk escarpment at Woolland Hill. By now his strength was failing and he lay down on Stoke Common, at Stoke Wake, where the hounds soon polished him off.

Mr Vansittart was then staying at Cattistock and had only one horse for his hunting needs. He was very fond of the sport and had been out up to three times a week. This seven-mile run settled his mount's fate for he dropped down dead just as the fox was killed. Mr Vansittart could ill afford a replacement hunter, so Mr Farquharson opened a subscription list, with much of the money being pledged then and there.

FRANTIC 40 MINUTES FROM FRANCE FARM ENDS AT BLANDFORD BREWERY

Meeting in the rain on Spetisbury Down, above the River Stour, on 9 March 1845, Mr Farquharson's Hounds needed an extended draw and took them miles. Having set off westwards, to Great Coll Wood, they went on to Whatcombe covers at Winterborne Whitechurch and then worked their way northwards across several parishes, in a great loop via Milton Park, Bully Wood and Park Coppice, to Oakhills, Houghton Wood, Field Grove and Bryanston Gallop, to reach the River Stour upstream from Blandford.

By now the hounds were heading homeward, when a labourer said that if they crossed the river and the valley to Mr Raxworthy's chalklands at France Farm he could promise them a brace of foxes in France Oaks. He was as good as his word and one ran away north-eastwards, nearly to Tarrant Gunville. Then it turned around, south-westwards, leaving Pimperne to the left, to Lord Portman's deer park and Blandford town. By the time the horses were approaching the Crown Hotel, the leading hounds were in sight of their fox. It swam the river beside the bridge and landed on the opposite bank with the hounds half-way across.

Then, after a brilliant run of six miles in just 40 minutes, they rolled him over by Lord Portman's lodge. Only the best-bred horses had been able to keep up with the frantic pace. A good 'holloa' came from Hector's Brewery (now Hall and Woodhouse), accompanied by hearty hospitality which ensured that everyone departed as happy as crickets. The inner man was well warmed even though shirts were wet through and boots full of rain-water.

THE GREAT HILTON DOWN RUN, OF TWENTY-FIVE MILES, MEETS RAILWAY NAVVIES AT DORCHESTER

It was on 26 April 1846 that Mr Farquharson's Hounds met for a meet at Bulbarrow in sleet and snow that would be recalled for the rest of the century. It was anything but a hunting morning and the old Squire was not out.

A fox was found in Balmers Coombe Bottom, below Rawlsbury Camp, and ran across into Melcombe Park where it went into a drain. It was decided to leave him there for another day. Colonel Bingham invited the horsemen to his old mansion for a lunch of bread and cheese with home-brewed two-year-old beer. It put them in good pluck for what was to follow.

Business resumed at two o'clock when the pack went up into the furze on the slope above the house, towards Hilton, and jumped a brace of foxes. The hounds caught a vixen, full of cubs, just going to lay down. Treadwell dismounted and threw her up on the hedge, as he put the hounds on the old dog, which had ten minutes' start.

They went down through Coombe Bottom and headed south-west across the Cheselbourne downs to West Bagber Copse, which he did not enter, and Milborne Wood. This was then all one cover as the central part had not yet been rooted out.

On he went, over the Puddletown-Blandford turnpike, with Jem Treadwell and Henry Symonds watching his crossing a 50-acre field on Milborne Farm, in the direction of Tolpuddle. He tried to enter big earths in Tolpuddle Eweleaze but these had been stopped up for a meet at Milborne Wood a few days before. He carried on southwards, crossing the road between Tolpuddle and Burleston, and the Piddle water-meadows, to Park Farm and Tincleton Hanging.

Still without a check, he then turned to the west, south of Cowpound, and crossed Ilsington Heath. He reached the top of Yellowham Wood but then heard some guns – rabbiting was taking place – and raced southwards again. He crossed Bhompston Heath and Duddle Heath to Norris Mill.

From here he went west, following the water-meadows along the north side of the River Frome, to West Stafford. Having crossed the river at Stafford House, into Mr Floyer's shrubbery, and over Stafford Eweleaze, where navvies were building the South-Western Railway from Southampton to Dorchester. 'They had not seen our fox,' Symonds said, 'and we went on to Winterborne Came where nearly every horse came to a trot.'

The hounds, meanwhile, were across Fordington Field and turning north, to keep the Weymouth road to the west and pass where Dorchester South Station now is. Their fox skirted the eastern side of Dorchester and Fordington, to Loud's Mill and eastwards again, to return to the water-meadows upstream from Stafford.

Treadwell saw an old hound hit the scent into a narrow hedgerow, with a brook on the other side, and the huntsman cheered as Druid kept up his deep note until he reached the end of the hedgerow. Druid and the fox then went into the brook together. Treadwell jumped off his horse and plunged into the water, up to his neck, to take the fox away from the single hound and throw him to the pack. They ate him up as stiff as a stick.

It had been a record run which was pronounced to be 25 miles – by agreement of Burgess, House and Fookes – during which they were never off his line, or changed. All the horses were tired, and after a much needed liquor-up, the field dispersed to the closest quarters that could be found for the evening. The hounds would not be back at Eastbury until ten o'clock that night.

WEYMOUTH ADMIRAL DROPS DEAD IN HIS TRACKS

When Mr Farquharson's Hounds met at Coker's Frome, Dorchester, on 4 December 1846 they found in Pigeon House Coppice and went away over Waterston Ridge and Piddlehinton Downs to Kingrove and Black Hill, where they killed in 35 minutes without a check. The downs were shrouded in hill fog and Mr Farquharson missed his huntsman, Jem Treadwell.

The whip who was sent to look for him returned with the sad news that Admiral Paine, from Weymouth, had dropped dead from his horse. The hounds were ordered home.

EIGHT MILES AN HOUR, FROM HIGHER WATERSTON TO ALTON PANCRAS

The morning after a County Ball in Dorchester, on 9 January 1847, Mr Farquharson's Hounds met at James Harding's farm, at Higher Waterston. They soon found a fox, in a hedgerow, and chased it almost the full length of the Old Sherborne Road, via Kingrove, Holcombe and Hawcombe, before turning south-eastwards to be killed in Alton Pancras parish. It was a run of 60 minutes, covering eight miles, without a check.

SIXTEEN-MILE RUN, FROM WINTERBORNE HOUGHTON TO MILBORNE PORT

Meeting in Houghton Wood, Winterborne Houghton, on 3 March 1847, Mr Farquharson's Hounds found, ran and changed many times before they emerged from that large cover. Then a fox broke away and made for Ibberton Park, sinking the hill and running for the heart of the Blackmore Vale. He went to Deadmoor Common and Rooksmoor and then headed north-west, leaving Stock House to the right, to the Caundle Holts and from there in a direct line for Milborne Port.

Here he entered the next county and went into a drain close to Sir William Medlycott's seat at Ven House. The time had been about 120 minutes and the distance 16 miles; the hounds had not required any help.

ZIG-ZAG COURSE UP THE PIDDLE VALLEY, TO SAFETY AT ARMSWELL

It was on 5 November 1847 – Guy Fawkes Day – that Mr Farquharson's Hounds met at Down House, above Bryanston. All the covers drew blank there and at Whitechurch Plantation, Peat Hill, and Horse Close. Using his local knowledge, Henry Symonds told Mr Farquharson that there had been an old fox lying in Warren Hill, on the ridge south of Milborne Wood, all the summer.

Treadwell was sent to draw it at once, as time was slipping along, and Penny, the whip, saw the fox heading southwards for Tolpuddle Common. Soon the pack were on his scent and rattled away to Burleston, where they entered the Piddle water-meadows and followed them around Admiston and Athelhampton into the mile-long valley stretching northwards up the Devil's Brook to Bason Hill. From here he headed north-west, across Druce Down, to Hill's Copse. He bore to the west over Muston Meadows to Burn Coppice and ran straight ahead over the flat, leaving Piddlehinton and Piddletrenthide villages to the left. This downland loop brought him to Dole's Ash where he turned westwards, to drop down into the valley beside Mr Bridge's home at the Manor House in Piddletrenthide.

He continued through the long plantation and across the downs above the east side of the valley, between Alton Pancras and Plush, and was visibly struggling about two fields ahead of the hounds. Treadwell was in hopes of handling him before he reached the safety of the big earths at the western end of the Armswell cover. Though they well deserved him, however, the hounds would be disappointed.

It had been a gruelling run of thirteen miles and the horses would not recover for some time. Henry Symonds was on his chestnut and Frederick House was riding Dainty. As the hounds wended their way back to Eastbury, Symonds and friends adjourned to the hospitality of James Davis at nearby Melcombe Horsey.

FOX CLIMBS A YEW TREE TO SAVE HIS BRUSH BESIDE ST GILES'S HOUSE

Close to home at Eastbury, Mr Farquharson's Hounds met at Crichel House on 7 December 1847, and ran for some time before they lost the scent. The order was given to head for Horton where they soon found and were off northwards without a turn to Wimborne St Giles and the covers at Cranborne. On they went, into the extremity of Dorset beyond the training ground of Woodyates Stables and to the south of Vernditch.

It had been a fast 75 minutes, quite possibly with a change of foxes, and after a ring a fox broke away across country in the direction of Queen's Coppice. Being headed, he then turned back to Cranborne Woods and St Giles's House. Here, opposite Lord Shaftesbury's home, the hounds lost their fox beneath a solitary yew tree in the grounds of this noble domain. It had been seen a few minutes before and everyone was puzzled by its disappearance.

The answer came at six o'clock, just after the hounds were out of sight, when a servant looked up into the tree and down came the fox. By now the stars were shining brightly and there was nothing that could be done. Classic cunning had saved his brush.

SHORT RUN ENDS IN CERNE ABBAS BUT THE WEATHER IS THE REAL WINNER

Having met at Melcombe Park on 9 January 1848, Mr Farquharson's Hounds soon found and went away to the north-west, over Monkwood Hill, and across the southern edge of the Blackmore Vale to Alton Common. They then headed south-west to cross Buckland Knoll and the Buckland Newton road and continued to Holcombe and went over the Old Sherborne Road, into Lord Digby's land at Minterne Magna where they turned south down the Cerne Valley, below the Cerne Giant, and killed in Cerne Abbas town after a sharp five-mile run.

Dispersing into sleet and snow, the horsemen then had to take on the weather which, in Henry Symonds' case, brought on rheumatic fever that had him confined to the house for two months and prevented any more hunting that season.

Quick eight miles, from Melcombe Park to Puddletown

Mr Farquharson's Hounds were back in Melcombe Park on 20 January 1849. The pack crossed the valley to Mr Davis' house and went up the long plantation, then across the open fields west of Cheselbourne, southwards to Dole's Hill, Furzey Down, Chebbard Farm, and Druce Down. They went on to Dewlish Warren and Bason Hill and crossed the Puddletown-Blandford turnpike, to follow the water-meadows to Athelhampton and Admiston Farm. They killed in Puddletown, close to Ilsington House, after a quick run of eight miles without a check. The hounds went back to Eastbury.

Nether Cerne to Hilfield, via Grimstone and Stratton

Meeting at Nether Cerne on 7 November 1849, Mr Farquharson's Hounds found in a furze-brake west of the farm and went on to run up and down the slopes of Grimstone and Stratton, two miles south-west. They then went up the valley of the Sydling Water to Sydling Clappers, and crossed over and down High Stoy, as if for Grange Woods at Middlemarsh.

Instead, he headed northwards into the Blackmore Vale, towards Totnell Corner, and entered Cockeram's Plantation at Leigh, then being killed in the open at Hilfield having gone ten miles and lost the strength to reach the large badger earths in Hanover Hanging Coppice.

The great Minterne run of twenty-five miles in sleet and snow

Bracing themselves for a taste of real winter, Mr Farquharson's Hounds met at Up Cerne Wood on 19 December 1849 and found immediately, going directly north-west to Batcombe, where they lost their fox. Returning along the escarpment to Minterne Magna they found again – a brace this time – one of which the pack killed.

Jem Treadwell caught a glimpse of the other fox, which looked like a traveller, and in this he was not mistaken. For the hounds were clapped on his line and went westwards through Up

Cerne to Sydling Wood, turning eastwards at the meadows, up the slope to the ridgeway and Cerne Park beyond. He left the former deer park to his left and headed down the valley, south-eastwards, to cross the Cerne-Dorchester turnpike at Nether Cerne. Here, the wind puffed out of him by the pace, he lay down in a chalkpit where Jem prepared to nab him.

Instead, he jumped up in full view, using the short respite to gather his second wind, and showed his agility by outrunning his pursuers in a northern course up the valley of the Cerne River to Up Cerne Park and Up Cerne Wood. Having been here before, and again tiring of the pace, he then turned back into the Cerne valley and returned to Cerne Abbas beside the Cerne Union Workhouse below the Giant and crossed the enclosures on the western side of the town, down to Godmanstone, where he crossed to the slopes of the Frome valley at Grimstone Down, and turned into that of the Sydling Water at Magiston water-meadows.

Here the field was coming to a standstill, with blown horses and diverse casualties resulting from the heavy work, as most horsemen wished he would not top the hill. This sturdy old customer was not to be handled yet, for over the hill he went, as fresh as a four-year-old, crossing the Dorchester-Yeovil turnpike and heading westwards across Frampton water-meadows. He set his head straight for the hills and reached East Compton.

'Ah,' said Jem. 'We shall have you my boy.' As if divining Jem's wicked intentions, he turned up across Compton Eweleazes, and the Roman Road, dropping down southwards into Winterbourne Abbas. There was a check and it seemed as if the pursuit was about to come to a close in some outhouse. Jem felt, or at least sought, for his pocket-knife to 'brush' him.

Then Barmaid hit off on the scent again, across the Dorchester-Bridport turnpike, and away went the pack again. They went through the Winterbourne plantations, straight over the downs for the Whatcombe earths, but, disdaining these, the gallant foe held his course by Kingston Russell House, across the water-meadows, as if for Foxholes Coppice, though he left this to the west. Instead he went around the great slopes to Winterbourne Long Plantation and turned again at Big Wood Lodge. He was now making for the laurels in Mr Williams' pleasure grounds at Bridehead House.

Here he was killed, after 130 minutes of the best run ever known in Dorsetshire, with a distance from point to point being 15 miles and some 25 miles in terms of the ground traversed by the hounds. Sleet and snow had been falling all the time in a piercing freezing wind.

FROM ROOKSMOOR TO HILTON, AND A BAD-TEMPERED ESCAPE

Mr Farquharson's Hounds met at Fifehead Neville on 5 January 1850 and found in Rooksmoor. They came away over nearby Deadmoor Common and left Hazelbury Bryan parish to the west, as they went across some of the stiffest Blackmore Vale countryside by Locketts Farm and on to Kitmore Coppice and Whitmore. Here Henry Symonds, riding a strange horse, took two falls. Next came Ibberton and Belchalwell, where there were bellows to mend, and most of the field led their horses up the challenging escarpment.

Having crossed Ibberton Down they turned through the woods at Delcombe Head and headed westwards down Balmers Coombe Bottom to Pleck and Ansty Brewery. Then they turned east, over Hilton Down to the plantation beside the parish church. Here the good fox was beat, after eleven miles, and lay down in the scrub. Jem Treadwell kept casting around, as Henry Symonds saw what he thought was the hunted fox slipping away into the field to the left. He reported this to Treadwell who insisted that it must have been a fresh fox. Tempers were lost and Symonds went home to Milborne St Andrew sure that their fox had been foolishly abandoned.

SPLIT PACK, TO BOTH ARMSWELL AND STALBRIDGE PARK

Meeting at Short Wood, Mappowder, on 13 January 1850, Mr Farquharson's Hounds disturbed a brace of foxes and split in two directions. James Penny, the whip, went with part of the pack and most of the field, southwards to Armswell Farm. Jem Treadwell, the huntsman, joined six couple of hounds that went away to the north-west, to Humber Wood and the River Lydden, passing between Pulham and the Green Man at King's Stag.

They then went north to Stock Woods, Stock House and Lydlinch Common. Crossing the brook they continued nearly to Thornhill and made their turn with the Blandford-Wincanton turnpike, to pass to the west of Stalbridge town into Stalbridge Park. Here, adjoining the next county at Landshire Lane, they lost their fox after nine miles.

FAST FOUR MILES, FROM BROADLEY WOOD TO CHARLTON DOWN

Meeting beside the River Stour at Hayward Bridge, Shillingstone, Mr Farquharson's Hounds had a disappointing morning on 27 January 1850. They climbed on to the hills at Escombe and got on the line of a fox which ran through Broadley Wood, southwards across Fairmile and on to the Down House plantations, through Little Wood, and then over the Blandford-Dorchester turnpike at Thornicombe. They followed him across Charlton Down to a small furze brake, beside Little Coll Wood, where they killed him after a very fast run of only four miles.

QUICK RUN FROM HOUGHTON WOOD TO THE STOUR RIVERBANK

Having met at Houghton Wood, Winterborne Houghton, on 23 February 1850, Mr Farquharson's Hounds went away to Turnworth and crossed the road into Bonsley Common, straight ahead across the open fields to Broadley, on to the Old Warren, and across the Stickland road close to Down House. Having run down from Fairmile to the Blandford-Dorchester turnpike, he crossed to the fields and meadows of Blandford St Mary, where he was killed on the west bank of the River Stour, opposite Langton House, after a quick six miles.

SOMERSET RUN ENDS IN DORSET AT CLIFTON MAYBANK

Meeting in the Somersetshire Holts and doing all the work themselves, Mr Farquharson's Hounds had a remarkable run of 105 minutes on 11 December 1852. It reached its conclusion by crossing the Dorset boundary at Clifton Maybank, south of Yeovil, and killing just short of Clifton Wood.

MR FARQUHARSON PAYS FOR CATS KILLED IN A PIDDLEHINTON COTTAGE

A meet in Milborne Wood, on 16 January 1853, had a rather unfortunate end for Mr Farquharson's Hounds, or rather their master. They followed a good scent across the fields to Dewlish Hangings and over the meadows by Dewlish House, then south-westwards through Dewlish Park and Warren Plantation, over the Cheselbourne road and Druce Downs, to Hill's Copse, Furzey Down, and Dole's Hill.

Here Reynard tried the earth, which had been blocked, and as the hounds closed on him, he took off over the fields into the middle of Piddlehinton parish where the door of a cottage happened to be open. A woman and her family were at lunch.

The fox rushed in, followed by the hounds, upsetting the table and everything on it. As well as the fox, the hounds killed two cats, and left the woman and her children frightened and distressed. They cried for the loss of their pussies. Mr Farquharson put his hand into his pocket and paid for the damage they had sustained. It had been a very fast run, of five miles, without a check.

HENRY STURT LEADS ALL THE WAY, FOR TEN MILES FROM CRICHEL

Breakfast at Crichel House started the day for followers of Mr Farquharson's Hounds on 4 February 1854. They found a good fox in the willow-bed and went away at a rattling pace, northwards into the next great estate at Wimborne St Giles, and on into Cranborne country. Henry Gerard Sturt (later Lord Alington) led all the way on his favourite bay mare. The fox went to ground in the main earth on Payne's Moor, without a check, after a good ten miles from point to point.

BRISK SIX MILES, FROM CHARMINSTER TO DRUCE DOWN

The Forston meet of Mr Farquharson's Hounds on 2 March 1854 turned into a bad morning going around Nether Cerne and Kingrove, towards Piddletrenthide, following which they found a straight-necked in Lord Ilchester's brake near Charminster. This went away over the downs to Wolfeton Clump, over Coker's Frome Farm, and northwards across Waterston Ridge to Higher Waterston Farm and Muston. It then crossed the Piddlehinton road to Barn Coppice and went up the Piddle meadows towards Dole's Hill and Druce Down, where he was pulled down without a check, after a brisk six miles.

SIX-MILE EVENING DASH, FROM MILTON PARK TO WOODBURY HILL

Meeting in Milton Park at the end of the season on 21 April 1855, Mr Farquharson's Hounds soon found but could not make a fox break away before five o'clock. The first runner of the day went through Lee Wood, Chescombe Farm, Longthorns and across the Blandford-Dorchester turnpike to Horse Close. He was crossing Bere Down to Kingston Clump when the huntsmen met a man returning home from his day's work.

Jem Treadwell asked if he had seen their fox. 'Yes', he said, 'about five minutes ago he was lapping some water out of the wheel-rut.' On went the hounds, to Muddox Barrow, and over the Bere-Wimborne turnpike to the corner of Woodbury Hill, where they ran into him just before reaching the big earths in Bere Wood. The hounds had been at work for seven hours and had just covered six miles.

SEVEN MILES, FROM HOUGHTON WOOD TO PIMPERNE, ENDS AT DUSK

Meeting at Bulbarrow on 8 January 1856, Mr Farquharson's Hounds found a fox in Delcombe Head and ran into Houghton Wood. Here there were several foxes on foot and they kept changing for two hours or more. Finally one broke away, after more than two hours, to Ibberton Park, Ibberton Down, Turnworth, and across the Okeford road to Bonsley Common, leaving Elcombe and Escombe covers to the east.

He was going over the Durweston farms in a line for Broadley, but then turned eastwards and ran down over Bryanston Gallop. He crossed the River Stour between France Farm and Nutford Farm. On the other side he went across the big down in the direction of Pimperne Bushes. It was now after four o'clock and getting dark but Jem Treadwell realised the hounds were running for blood. Henry Symonds then came across their fox, lying full-length in a deep wheel-rut, and beckoned to Jem that the hounds had over-run the scent.

Independently, the hounds threw up their heads, and made a cast back. Up jumped Charlie, into their mouths, as a well deserved reward after seven miles at the end of a long day.

PUZZLING LAST TWENTY MINUTES OF A FOX RUNNING SHORT

Meeting on Eggardon Hill, on the last bastion of the chalk massif above Bridport, Mr Farquharson's Hounds found in Nallers, a favourite spinney, on 28 February 1856. Off they went, up the Askerswell valley, and on over the steep slopes at Stancombe, eastwards over the downs of Litton Cheney on the northern side of the Bridport-Dorchester turnpike. They continued to Compton Gore and followed the Roman Road for two miles.

Then they turned north, over Frampton Hogleaze, to Skippet Farm, where he began to twist and turn from under one hedge, across a field, down another hedge, then across a road for some distance. At last they pulled him down at the corner of Bradford Plantation. Treadwell had never found himself so puzzled with a fox running short than in those almost static twenty minutes at the end of ten miles of movement.

It would prove to be one of the last memorable runs for Mr Farquharson who admitted feeling his age and decided to give up his kennels in 1858. His country was divided in four parts in 1859. Lord Portman, who had stopped hunting through ill health in 1843, revived his pack and took the eastern portion. Testimonials were presented to Mr Farquharson in 1827, with the substantial sum of £1150 being raised, and at the end of fifty years' mastership, in 1857, when the £1800 collected paid for the commissioning of a portrait of the Master by (Sir) Francis Grant. Mr Farquharson was featured on his favourite horse, Botanist, with Rarity – one of the best hounds in his pack – at his side.

Jem Treadwell, who was as old as the century but would make return visits to his old country at other meets, had been Mr Farquharson's huntsman for twenty years. He came after the debacle following the madness of Mr Hall who lost half his pack in 1836 and replaced them by buying out Mr Codrington's South Wiltshire Hounds, bringing Jem Treadwell and family with them. That merely reinforced a failure and Henry Hall resigned at the end of the season, selling a portion of the pack – with Treadwell as part of the package – to Mr Farquharson, and the remainder to Mr Tudway of Wells. Jem Treadwell arrived at Eastbury Kennels with the hounds on 18 April 1837. He had two sons, who followed him into the sport; Tom Treadwell was first whipper-in to Lord Scarsdale's pack at Kedleston, Derbyshire, and second son Jack became huntsman to the Quorn. Treadwell's brother, Charles, was huntsman with the Bramham Moor Hounds.

Before Jem Treadwell, Ben Jennings had done thirty years' service. For half a century, with just those two legendary huntsmen, Mr Farquharson had reigned supreme in Dorset.

His Victorian statistics survive, from the Queen's accession in 1837, until the close of the 1857 season. These show a total of 2787 days hunted, during which 2688 foxes were killed, and 624 earthed. After deduction of twelve blank days, the 3312 foxes accounted for amounted to an average of better than a fox a day, with 25 foxes per season being the remainder in long division.

James John Farquharson, painted by Sir Francis Grant
and engraved by James Scott, in 1858.

'The Squire of Langton,' James John Farquharson, from a portrait of about 1810.

Squire Farquharson's western outpost, being his 'hunting box'
at Cattistock, from a contemporary watercolour.

Cattistock Kennels, established by James John Farquharson, in a contemporary watercolour.

Solomon Baker, the whipper-in of Mr Farquharson's Hounds, from 1806 to 1837.

Ben Jennings, huntsman to James John Farquharson from 1808 until 1837,
in a portrait issued as a print.

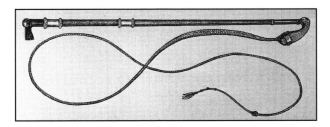

Ben Jennings' whip.

Military portrait, presented to Captain James John Farquharson in 1841
by members of his Blandford Independent Troop of the Dorset Regiment of
Yeomanry Cavalry, from a painting by Robert Say.

James ('Jem') Treadwell, the huntsman of
Mr Farquharson's Hounds from 1837,
photographed on his retirement in 1858.

Chapter Four

MR YEATMAN'S HOUNDS

MR YEATMAN'S PACK AT STOCK HOUSE

What would become famous in fox-hunting as the Blackmore Vale country, overlapping a medieval deer forest with occasional ancient oaks and expanses of wild commons surviving from the older landscape, was hunted at its heart by the Rev. Captain Harry Farr Yeatman R.N. (1791–1884). His estate, around Stock House at Stock Gaylard, included Lydlinch Common and still has its individualistic 'Y'-style farm gates on every field.

With John Channing as huntsman, and Joe Mitchel – one of the hardest riders of the day – as whip, Mr Yeatman's Hounds were established in 1826. They were dwarf foxhounds and chiefly hunted hare, plus the occasional fox and roe deer, across a territory that extended northwards, deep into Somerset. Mr Yeatman boasted in an after-dinner speech that his boundaries ranged:

> 'From the woods at the back of Stock
> To the alpine heights of Mendip,
> From the Pillar of renowned Hood
> to the Tower of immortal Alfred.'

It was a country of contrasts in terms of both cover and foxes. At one extreme, there was hardly a covert of any description between Yeovil and Compton Castle, whereas the ridge from Stourhead to Longleat was one colossal covert, and so full of earths that it would defeat the most vigilant earth-stopper. As for deepest Dorset; persecution of foxes was rife.

Despite the difficulties, meets became a sporting institution, with 285 horsemen gathering at Stock House in 1828 and 'after a brilliant burst of forty minutes they killed their fox in superior style in the open, before he could reach Caundle Holt coverts.' Another documented run, in March 1831, from the Somerset Batcombe, near Bruton, to the Mendip Hills, was logged at 25 miles in 240 minutes and ended with fox and hound sinking into a stream in a rocky gorge near Frome. It was a 'curious chase, which extended through 13 parishes', it being a peculiarity of Mr Yeatman's descriptions that he always noted the number of parishes hounds had been through.

Mr Yeatman discontinued hunting with his own hounds, after the death of John Channing, in 1833.

Chapter Five

MANSEL-PLEYDELL'S ROEBUCK HOUNDS

HEADING HOME WITH MANSEL-PLEYDELL'S BUCK-HOUNDS

 Edmund Mansel-Pleydell, of Whatcombe House at Milborne St Andrew, established a pack of Roebuck Hounds. They were kept at the Manor House in the village with William Rice as the huntsman. His tombstone, at Milborne, claims perhaps rather extravagantly that he was the first man ever to have hunted a pack of such hounds.

They closed their 1827–28 season on 5 April 1828. It was a brilliant day's sport. They threw off at Elcombe Wood, and in about ten minutes a fine buck was viewed going over the opposite hill, for Escombe, and made for Turnworth.

Then it broke out of the woods, over the lip of the downs at Bell Hill, and descended into the Blackmore Vale at Ibberton. Headed by some labourers, he went up the slope and skirted Ibberton Park, into Houghton Wood, where he passed through an extensive covert and turned through the enclosures of Mr M. Davis to a coppice at some distance to the north-east, near Durweston.

From here he headed for home, towards Elcombe, and attempted the hill. It was beyond his failing strength. He had to give up and turn back into the covert, breaking out the other side, but the whole pack (with the exception of one couple of hounds) ran into him, in view, in a short furze brake on the down. It had been a run of 100 minutes, without a single check, at good speed across mainly open country.

Chapter Six

THE MOUNTAIN HARRIERS

OUT WITH THE MOUNTAIN HARRIERS AT PIDDLEHINTON

James Harding kept and hunted a pack of Mountain Harriers at Higher Waterston, in the Piddle Valley, upstream from Puddletown. On 8 November 1830 they met at Almshouse Farm, Piddlehinton, and found a hare which was killed after a run of thirty minutes. In drawing for a second hare, through some turnips, they roused a noble fallow deer – a most unusual quarry – which launched away southwards over a tremendous rasper (a difficult fence), with the pack at its haunches, across the open common fields of Piddlehinton, crossing the brook at Muston farmhouse, over the hill to Waterston Farm, into Grey's Wood and then eastwards into Yellowham Wood.

The chase held on without a check, across the Dorchester-Puddletown turnpike, and south over the heath to Duddle. Turning westwards, from Bockhampton, he went through Kingston Maurward Park, and then having cleared the fence of a willow-bed, proceeded to cross numerous minor streams as well as the main flow of the River Frome. The pack gallantly swam the same. Southwards he went, through the water-meadows to West Stafford, up the hills to Knighton House, then on at the same pace towards Warmwell.

It was now evident that victory was to crown this incomparable pack's efforts. They ran into their quarry near Charlmont House, Broadmayne, where the select few who enjoyed this brilliant run were regaled by Mr Balston, the owner, whose name as a sportsman stood high. The distance was ten miles, over a variety of country, and the buck had been chased for 71 minutes.

FOX, HARES AND A ROE BUCK ALL IN ONE DAY

Another grand day's sport with the Mountain Harriers took place on 19 March 1831. Having met at Buckland Knoll, Buckland Newton, they ran through the heart of the Blackmore Vale. The first scent and sighting was a fox which was killed after a short chase.

Then a hare was followed, towards Beaulieu, and into Mappowder parish with Short Wood to the north and the village across to the south. It then crossed the stream into the parish of Hazelbury Bryan. Climbing the slope and passing the church it went on to skirt the covers on the north side of Cockcrow Copse. Then it led the pack into the fourth parish of what had become, for a hare, one of the best runs ever known in the Blackmore Vale. They ran into the little Jack hare, not much bigger than a rabbit, on reaching the church at Fifehead Neville. It had been a run of at least eight miles as the crow flies and had taken 55 minutes. The hounds were given their hare.

Another was found near Mappowder church and headed for the escarpment, through two small covers at Monkwood Hill, and into Melcombe Hill, where she was run into after a chase of 35 minutes.

Next for the staunch little pack was a roe deer. The buck remained elusive for an hour but then broke out of his cover and shot away over the meadows, then uphill to Melcombe Barn, and on to Lyscombe Hill. From here he took to the valley for Ball Wood and attempted to return to the hill covers. He was killed on the hill opposite Melcombe House, after running two hours. Rev. Harry Farr Yeatman, from Stock Gaylard House at Lydlinch, was out with the pack to the last and said it was the best day's sport he ever saw with the Harriers. It matched that with foxhounds, on the occasion they killed three dog foxes, having had really good runs with each.

FALLOW DOE RUNS FROM DEWLISH TO BERE REGIS

On New Year's Day in 1833 the Mountain Harriers met at Dewlish Turnpike Gate and found a fallow deer, a mottled doe, in Milborne Wood. She ran over open country, south-eastwards, for 55 minutes until the hounds were stopped, with difficulty, after it had entered Bere Wood, above Bere Regis.

QUICK HOUR ENDS BESIDE THE DINING ROOM OF CAME HOUSE

On the other hand, some runs could be memorable for their shortness or where they ended, with both being the case on 19 January 1833 when the Mountain Harriers met at West Stafford. First they found and lost their hare in the water-meadows. Then they discovered a fox on Woodsford Heath, near Hurst, and were almost hanging on his brush, as he crossed ploughed fields on Woodsford Farm. Reynard proceeded through the bogs, on to Lower Woodsford and Mr Kerslake's farm, and the strong furze and big plantations at Lewell and Stafford.

Bearing away to the east, leaving West Knighton to the south, he crossed the Dorchester-Wareham turnpike and went through the big eweleazes and large plantations into Came Park. Then he was in the shrubberies around Came House and into its back yards. He entered the blacksmith's shop and its doors were closed, to leave Reynard safe for another day, but he was too devious for his own good.

Having found a small hole under the bellows, he was out in the garden and round by Winterborne Came church to the gravel paths of Came House. Then he tried an underground drain but ended up in an open water gutter. The Master of Hounds gave him notice to quit and the harriers killed under the window of the dining room. It had been a quick sixty minutes.

TWO FALLOW DOES KILLED IN STOCK HOUSE COVERS

On the evening of 16 October 1833 the Mountain Harriers went north from Waterston with Travers, the whip, to Stock House, Lydlinch. The following morning, at the invitation of Rev. Harry Farr Yeatman, they met at 10.30 to hunt fallow deer. Conditions were wet and blustery.

Unfortunately the old buck they were in hopes of finding had been killed by poachers, on Bagber Common, a few days before. Having found a doe, the pack stuck to her most merrily, and took her in forty minutes without leaving her haunts.

Their second doe, in another half hour, only left the covers once. That was a brief excursion, and then the Bramley covers were traversed, again and again. They killed her in 90 minutes. The huntsmen dined and slept at Stock House and intended going out with Mr Yeatman the next day but it was too wet for sport.

GAME FALLOW DOE SPARED BY THE REVELS INN FIELD

Another deer hunt by the Mountain Harriers was from Revels Inn, near the northern end of the Old Sherborne Road, between the escarpment and Middlemarsh, on 11 November 1835. Sixty horsemen were out and the Mountain Harriers found almost immediately, in Mount Silver, and took away through Aldermoor Coppice to Dogbury Gate and over the hills, through Minterne Magna plantations and arable field to Giant's Head. Bearing around the top of Yelcombe Bottom and crossing the former turnpike, the Old Sherborne Road, it went over the eweleazes of Alton Pancras and down into the next valley, southwards to Piddletrenthide. Here it turned westwards above the church and headed over the downs to the plantations on Cerne Hill.

It then made for Kingrove, where at 55 minutes and with the wish of the field, the hounds were stopped; it was the same deer which they had found at Stoke Wake, two years before.

TIME RUNS OUT FOR THE BUCK OF HETHFELTON

On 14 December 1835, by invitation of eccentric Charborough Park squire and Wareham M.P. John Samuel Wanley Sawbridge Erle Drax (1800–87), the Mountain Harriers met at Broomhill Mill, near Woolbridge. They drew for a roebuck which had been seen in a willow-bed a week before.

Not having found, the gallant little pack went on to Hethfelton Plantation, an immense wild cover, where they drew until two o'clock. Then a cheery cry announced that this solitary animal was roused and the pack soon gave him notice to quit his stronghold. Going away over the wild heath, east towards Wareham, he made a northward turn towards Lower Hyde and then westwards to cross the rugged heath again, to return into Hethfelton. This time he left Hethfelton House to the south and went northwards, in the direction of Higher Hyde, and the romantic country to Gallows Hill. Thence he went over the bogs and Chamberlayne's Heath, and westwards through the fir clumps to Moreton Heath Lodge. Then he turned north, via Briantspuddle dairy-house, to cross the enclosures to the water-meadows, pointing for Kite Hill and Piddle Wood.

Up to this time he had been moving apace, without a check, but having crossed the River Piddle the buck covered himself among some spears. Dislodged from this cool retreat he took away over the meadows but the pack gradually closed and ran into him, after 72 minutes. The buck was given to Mr Fyler, of Hethfelton House.

PACK AHEAD OF THE HORSEMEN FOR SEVEN MILES

On 16 December 1835 the Mountain Harriers met at Bulbarrow and at once found a brace of deer. One took away southwards to the Lord's Wall with three-and-a-half couple of hounds. The other, with 13 couple following, went the other way and sank into the Blackmore Vale, by Norwood, to Mappowder Church, leaving Short Wood and the other covers to the north, and Melcombe Park to the south, as he made for Armswell Farm and the Dorsetshire Gap. No horseman caught up with the hounds for seven miles.

Then, crossing Alton Common to Buckland Knoll, the hounds were stopped at a brook. On casting they got on a hare and then a brace of foxes. Being on foot, the field lost their deer, which they hoped would provide another good run some day.

THE DAY LOST TO SNOW AT ANSTY

The Mountain Harriers had been due to meet at Hartfoot Lane, near Ansty Brewery, on 3 February 1836. Owing to the heavy fall of snow the previous day they could not hunt. Mail-coaches were stopped and many lives lost. The oldest people never remembered so much snow fall in so short a time. Travellers heading towards Dorset from Salisbury Plain were trapped on Charnage Down, above Mere, for three days.

ROE DOE RECEIVES HER LIBERTY AS THE REWARD FOR TWENTY MILES

A record distance for deer hunting in Dorset would be achieved by the Mountain Harriers on 13 February 1836. They met at Revels Inn and found their roe doe under Mount Silver. She bounded over the hill to the Minterne Magna plantations, then sunk into the vale by Clinger Farmhouse, and away at best pace by Grange Woods to High Stoy, through the Nursery gardens at Hermitage, skirting Hilfield Coppice, and over the steeps to Up Cerne Wood.

Here, after taking a refreshing dip in a pond, she turned short to the east, retracing part of the Up Cerne cover, and stretching over the hill to take the vale by Aldermoor, leaving Woolcombe Clump to the north, to Paper Hill Copse. From here the fences were thick and strong to Leigh Common. She crossed the turnpike road at Totnell Corner, and went by Whitehouse and Stockbridge Common, to Holnest Bushes and Small Farm, leaving Whitfield Wood to the west, pointing to Leweston House. Turning short to the south, the hounds got a view as the deer cleared tremendous raspers, heading towards Holnest Common, with the pack closing at her haunches.

A friendly check ensued, to give the blown nags a rest, but it was a short respite. Once again the 'little invincibles' were topping quick-set hedges at a merry pace. Having crossed the brook to Holnest Coppice, leaving Holnest House to the south, the doe crossed the enclosures by the church, taking the river and swimming under the bridge. She was discovered further down the Cam.

Some men attempted stopping the hounds from taking her but she then broke away, crossing the enclosures, and was finally taken uninjured in the turnpike road opposite Dunn's Farm, after 170 minutes of severe running for both horse and hound as the most arduous lover of the chase could wish to share. It had covered more than twenty miles, with the second half being through the stiffest and most difficult part of the Blackmore Vale, including much gorse.

Consequently, the field of 40 diminished to 15 stalwarts at the close – who spared their doe as a reward for her endeavours.

She was returned to Mount Silver later in the day. The Mountain Harriers would be back, however, to claim this doe on 15 April as their eighth and final roe deer of the 1836 season, by which time they had killed at total of 103 hares.

HILL-CLIMBING ROE DOE ESCAPES IN A HURRICANE

The Mountain Harriers met at Revels Inn, on 5 April 1836, to hunt roe deer. It was a good meet of upwards of 60 horsemen in the field, with 14 and a half couple of hounds. Mount Silver drew blank but a doe was found at two o'clock in Eight Acre Coppice, Buckland Newton. She was headed by people from one cover to the other before breaking away, by Revels Inn, upwards to Dogbury Gate and High Stoy Woods, then southwards to Up Cerne coppices.

Here she turned, pointing towards the vale, and descended to Hilfield. Turning again, westwards, she went through the dense alders beside the Wriggle River to Batcombe. Then she tackled the escarpment, up and over to Sydling Wood, and onwards to Woolcombe Clump.

By now, with the wind blowing a hurricane and the rain falling in torrents, hounds and horses were fairly beaten. It had been a run of 95 minutes. She was the same doe as had been taken and spared at Stoke Wake, after 110 minutes, three years before. Three other times were recalled, including an extraordinary run of 125 minutes, when she crossed the Blackmore Vale.

BULBARROW BUCK GIVEN TO CAPTAIN LOFTUS OF WOOLLAND HOUSE

Thick hill-fog prevented the Mountain Harriers, meeting at Hartfoot Lane on 12 April 1836, from heading for Bulbarrow. Hartfoot Lane, at Bingham's Melcombe, takes its name from the legendary deer which escaped from Windsor Park in the time 'when Julius Caesar reigned King'. It is commemorated in the sign of the King's Stag, between Pulham and Lydlinch, and its maypole marks the spot where the royal deer was taken.

They returned to Hartfoot Lane the following day and found three deer in Stoke Wood, above Stoke Wake. The buck led them eastwards, through Woolland Wood, then went over the hill to Ochill Barn and Houghton Stubbs, where the hounds worked him in fine style.

He then broke away for Milton Park but was headed, back towards Houghton Wood, where he was worried and killed. It had been a chase of 65 minutes, without check, at a first-rate pace. The three-year-old deer was given to Captain Loftus of Woolland House.

SAD END TO THE LONG-DISTANCE DOE AT MELBURY HOUSE

The Mountain Harriers returned to Revels Inn on 15 April 1836 to hunt the noted barren roe doe. The field of upwards of 130 horsemen and 100 on foot watched the uneventful drawing of Mount Silver and Grange Woods. Then word came that their deer was in Up Cerne Wood. Arriving there, and finding immediately beside the keeper's lodge, they were off at half-past two o'clock.

She pointed westwards for Sydling Wood but then turned north, striking the hill to Batcombe, and into the Blackmore Vale, through Aldermoors, and at a clinking pace to Paper Hill Coppice and the Leigh Commons, then over the stiff enclosures to Holnest Common, and south-west from Totnell Corner, parallel to Leigh and Chetnole, to cross that fine part of the vale that rises into Bubb Down Hill.

Here she entered into Melbury Woods, belonging to the Earl of Ilchester, and jumped the iron fence into the deer park. Mr Harding stopped the hounds at 115 minutes. Their deer was dead-beat after a distressing pace for the horses and hounds of at least 18 miles. Some people caught the deer under the windows of Melbury House but she escaped and attempted to jump a wall 12 feet high. She unfortunately fell back and broke her back.

There was another casualty. Mr Harry Nash, riding his favourite grey steeplechaser with a 'boot' on one of his fore-legs, in taking a double hedge found a stake between the 'boot' and the leg, causing the horse to fall into the opposite ditch and break its neck. Mr Nash was the noted Dorchester veterinary surgeon. He died in the town's cholera outbreak of 1849. The hounds had 14 miles to return home. Mr Harding gave three-quarters of this deer to Mr H. Digby and the other quarter to Mr Spinks of Melbury.

RAIN SAVES THE HARTFOOT LANE BUCK

The Mountain Harriers met at Hartfoot Lane, Bingham's Melcombe, on 9 March 1837. They drew blank in the cover by the Red House and went up to Stoke Wood. Two does were with a buck, which took multiple turns, before breaking away over the hill beside Stoke Church, through Balmers Combe Bottom, and across the stiff corner of the Blackmore Vale to Melcombe Park. After making a south-westerly turn in that stronghold, it took to the hills by Nettlecombe Tout and the eweleazes.

He passed to the north of the Fox Inn at Plush (the hamlet now has the Brace of Pheasants, and our Fox Inn is to be found to the east, at Lower Ansty). The buck went on to Ball Wood and Armswell but then turned back, over Plush Hill to Watcombe Wood, and sank through Plush Bottom to the Folly.

Beat by rain, hail and the wind, the chase was halted at 110 minutes.

CHARBOROUGH ROE-BUCK TAKEN IN LYTCHETT HIGH WOOD

The Mountain Harriers met at Charborough Lodge on 11 March 1838. They found a fine roe-buck in a nearby plantation, and palings were removed to encourage him to break away over the road, rather than across the park. He chose the latter, however, and ran through elements of the herd of nearly 600 fallow deer.

Skirting these, and running through the park gates which were thrown open, the buck went away through the plantations and enclosures to Lytchett High Wood, which he refused to leave, and where he was finally taken after standing before the hounds. It had been a chase of 68 minutes.

STICKING TO THEIR BUCK, IN DELCOMBE BOTTOM, FOR 65 MINUTES

On 19 April 1838 the Mountain Harriers met at Delcombe Wood, by permission of Mr Damer of Milton Abbey, and made another bold attempt to hunt a deer. They found about a dozen, running in all directions, and singled out a buck. He never left the extensive Delcombe Bottom covers where the little hounds stuck to their quarry for 65 minutes. They then killed their buck to the admiration and astonishment of the whole field.

BULBARROW TO PIDDLES WOOD AND ALMOST BACK AGAIN

The Mountain Harriers met at Bulbarrow on 13 December 1838, with twelve-and-a-half couple of hounds. They found a brace of deer immediately and a fine old buck broke away from the hillside covers, westwards into Woolland Ivors, with Delcombe Woods to the south, and ran over the hills to Hilton Woods, then bearing south for Milton Abbas covers. Here the hounds had to be stopped, after 40 minutes, due to many deer being on the move.

The hounds were taken back to Stoke Wood, above Stoke Wake, and found a brace more. They settled on a four-year-old doe and having run the covers for some time then crossed over to Norwood. Having gone straight through this long cover they broke away northwards across the Blackmore Vale and passed to the east of the parish church at Hazelbury Bryan. Here the fences became very strong and tested the nerves.

The little hounds were now pointing for Piddles Wood, beyond Sturminster Common, at a merry pace. Having run from scent into view they obliged her to turn around. She now headed back towards the hills, south to Woolland Wood, and went straight through one corner. She was breaking for Woolland Common but was run into in a small plantation after 113 minutes and ten miles. The deer was given to Captain Loftus of Woolland House.

Venison sent from Hilton Woods to Park Lane

The Mountain Harriers met at Hartfoot Lane, Bingham's Melcombe, on 30 December 1838. As before, they were hunting roe deer, and found a buck. They gave him a good rattling into the Blackmore Vale covers and then back over the hills to Hilton Woods, where having given him several turns, they killed in 30 minutes. The buck, by the wish of Major Shirley, was sent to Colonel the Honourable G.L.D. Damer, Master of Hounds, at No. 6 Tilney Street, Park Lane, London.

James Harding kept precise records and would send for stuffing the thousandth hare that was killed by his merry pack.

Chapter Seven

THE PORTMAN HOUNDS

LORD PORTMAN'S HOUNDS, OUT FROM BRYANSTON

Edward Berkeley (1799–1888), became the head of the wealthy Portman family after his father died suddenly, on a mission to Rome, in 1823. He reluctantly agreed to enter politics, succeeding his father as county Member of Parliament for Dorset, and applied himself with more pleasure to the management of vast estates, including Bryanston House, near Blandford, and the much more lucrative Marylebone 'Village' in what is now central London. There his father had employed architect Joseph Parkinson to create Bryanston Square and Montagu Square (1810–15), with the latter being remembered for the Mrs Montagu who found a young chimney sweep descending into her boudoir and promptly put him to good use between the sheets.

At home, Edward Berkeley would adopt the Portman name and be remembered as Lord Portman, though he was not created Baron Portman of Orchard Portman until 1837, and this would be superseded by the title of first Viscount Portman of Bryanston in 1873. By 1834, with Kit Atkinson as his huntsman, Edward Berkeley turned Bryanston into a focal point for country sport, establishing what would soon be known as Lord Portman's Hounds and became the Portman Hunt.

Mr Portman had taken on the mastership of the Blackmore Vale Hounds in the 1830–31 season and continued until 1840 when he handed over to Henry Hall and sold his pack to Mr Drax of Charborough. Then, having assembled another pack, Lord Portman hunted the Houghton country until 1843, when a serious illness caused him to give up, selling his hounds to the Earl of Shannon.

The Bryanston pack would be revived, however, after Mr Farquharson ceased hunting in 1858. The following year the eastern quarter of his country was given to Lord Portman. He retained his old servant, John Donniscombe, as huntsman until 1862. He was succeeded by John Smith.

66

His lordship's son and heir, Henry William Berkeley, the second Viscount Portman, continued the Portman Hunt after his father's death in 1888 with Joe Moss as huntsman.

EIGHTEEN MILES FROM YEATMAN COUNTRY TO DRUCE

One of the best of Mr Portman's early runs was from Stock Gaylard House, the home of Rev. Harry Farr Yeatman, near Lydlinch. A fox was found in Stock covers and broke away over the River Lydden to Deadmoor Common and Rooksmoor, heading west to the Green Man at King's Stag. From here he went southwards to Humber Wood and Cannings Court, then across the enclosures to Short Wood, north-west of Mappowder, from where he put his head straight for Melcombe Park. Having gone through this big cover without turn, he ascended Nettlecombe Tout and crossed the high downs between Lyscombe and Plush, to pass to the east of Dole's Ash House. They then raced him over the open country to Cheselbourne Down and into Druce Down, north-west of Puddletown, where they pulled down this 'Vale and Hill' fox after 18 miles.

MILTON PARK CUSTOMER FAILS UNDER THE CERNE GIANT

Another long-remembered meet was at Milton Park, where they took on an old customer who had twice lost them at Bulbarrow. This time Mr Edward Portman, as he was then known, told Kit Atkinson not to let the hounds draw, but to go through the middle track with his horn blaring. One of the whips was sent on to the top of the cover to keep look-out. The hounds were half-way through this big wood when their fox broke away over the Winterborne Stickland road.

Atkinson got on his line and rattled him along to Bully Wood, Park Coppice, and on up Delcombe, all the way to Delcombe Head, being the chalkland side of Bulbarrow. This time, however, they kept him going, across the Ansty road, down through Balmers Coombe Bottom.

Reynard then went over the Hazelbury Bryan road and across that stiff bit of vale into Melcombe Park, going straight through this immense wood without a turn. On emerging he headed on to Spring's Coppice, leaving Ansty to the east and Plush to the south, as he went into Armswell long cover. He broke away at the far end, westwards by Bookham Farm, and crossed the Buckland Newton road, straight on to Holcombe and Giant's Head. From here he turned left, by the side of the former turnpike, following the Old Sherborne Road southwards for a mile. Then he turned west down Yelcombe Bottom, for his final mile and a last turn, northwards from Cerne town, to be killed under where the Cerne Giant is cut out of the side of the hill. He had made 12 miles.

QUICK FIVE MILES, FROM LYDLINCH TO SHERBORNE PARK

One of the notable quick sprints from one country house to the next took place on 21 January 1836, when the Portman Hounds met at Lydlinch Bridge, and headed west to draw Rev. Harry Farr Yeatman's cover in Stock Wood. A fox was found immediately and soon departed the vicinity of Stock Gaylard House for the valley of the Caundle Brook and onwards at a racing pace for five miles into Lord Digby's Sherborne Park. Here, however, he escaped in a foil of deer, obstacles, and other impediments, in the beautiful setting of Jerusalem Hill, overlooking the two castles and Sherborne Lake.

TEN MILES IN 100 MINUTES, ENDING AT PLUSH

On 9 February 1836, Edward Berkeley found his first fox for the day on the downs near his own cover of Broadley Wood, above Bryanston, and killed in 40 minutes. Then he found his second in Field Grove, his favourite cover, and Reynard tried every point near home, making his way through the pleasure grounds of Bryanston House. He then dashed through the River Stour with the pack at his heels. The hounds were somewhat thrown out by the iron rails of the fence around the deer park, with the fox slipping through and taking to the open downs towards the great Cranborne Chase, but the gallant beauties still pressed on. They ran into their fox in open view, in such style as would not be forgotten by those who had the pleasure of being present.

On 11 February 1836 they found their fox in the Blackmore Vale, in Woolland Wood, and made play over the steep escarpment for Milton Abbey covers. Then he turned westwards, for the valley leading into Melcombe Park, through this strong and extensive cover, before going over the hill at a racing pace across the downs of Plush and Piddletrenthide. He then entered King's Grove Bottom, to the west of the village, but was brought down in the open after covering a good ten miles, in 100 minutes.

TWELVE MILES, FROM KING'S STAG TO DUNCLIFFE HILL

The Portman Hounds met on 15 February 1836 in the heart of the Blackmore Vale, at Rooksmoor, on the east side of the River Lydden at King's Stag. They got away directly with a brace of foxes and sent the old dog eastwards to Deadmoor and along the enclosures by Lydlinch Bridge and Bagber Common. Onward at a rattling pace for the Stour meadows, and across the river, north-eastwards into Hinton Coppices.

Here the pack transferred to a fresh fox but were soon put right and off again after the wily old customer. He had a reputation for defeating his followers around this spot. This time was different, and never did hounds go along in such splendid style, in a solid square, as they worked their way through the Marnhull Valley to Moorside and the deep grassy fields of Margaret Marsh and West Stour, followed by the 400 acres of Duncliffe Wood. He reached it just before the hounds and strove to find the big earths but old Limner turned him, and the pack closed in for the kill. It was another run of 100 minutes, to within sight of Shaftesbury, with a distance of over 12 miles.

MORE FROM THE NEVER-FAILING YEATMAN COVERS

The Portman Hounds met at Town Bridge, Sturminster Newton, on 26 February 1836 and set off northwards to draw the Hinton St Mary covers. These proved blank. So they went on to Stock Gaylard where they were more fortunate and found directly. After a turn or two they broke away across the Blackmore Vale, for Rooksmoor and Deadmoor Common, and headed for Haydon, where they turned into the open commons and enclosures on the banks of the Lydden, leaving Stock Woods to the north, and headed westwards to Caundle Brook and the Caundle Holts beyond it. Here the scent became poor.

It had been a good run, of 75 minutes, and landowner Harry Farr Yeatman was complimented, for the second time in a week, on providing sport from his never-failing covers. It was calculated that in the past two seasons and a half, drawing them 27 times, a total of 26 foxes had been found.

EXCITING TWELVE MILES, FROM MILTON PARK TO WAREHAM

A Milton Park meet of the Portman Hounds in March 1836 found another straight-necked fox but he would run in an entirely different direction from the last runner from this venue. He broke away south-eastwards to Whatcombe and La Lee covers, on to Chescombe Farm and over the Blandford-Dorchester turnpike, across the middle of Mr Fookes' farm at Winterborne Whitechurch, and over the open downs – not cultivated in those days – to Kingston fir-clump and through Muddox Barrow, the parish of Bere Regis. Then he crossed the Bere-Wimborne turnpike, still bearing south-east, into Bere Wood and on to the Bloxworth covers, where he turned south on Bloxworth Green.

Next he crossed the road leading from Bere Regis to Lytchett and Poole, into open heathland for a mile, to the ancient encampment of Woolsbarrow which is known as Pickard's Lookout, from its associations with the local and learned Pickard-Cambridge family. Still he forged ahead, over the wild and boggy country to the west of Drax's Decoy and Morden Bog, with

Hyde Higher Lodge to the right. He crossed Trigon Hill and went on for his final mile, to the side of the Wareham-Poole road, at the point where the railway and Wareham Station now stand. It had been a good 12 miles, in a straight line.

LORD PORTMAN'S 'SCRATCH PACK' PASSES MUSTER

Lord Portman resumed hunting with a fresh pack of hounds for the 1858–59 season and met on 15 January 1859, at Houghton Wood, Winterborne Houghton. John Donniscombe was the huntsman. There were several foxes on foot and the hounds kept changing for some time before one broke away northwards over the down, through Ibberton Wood, to Ibberton Down, and eastwards to Turnworth. They crossed the Okeford road, into Bonsley Common, where they turned south-east, to run through Escombe and Elcombe – following breast-high scent up and down through the small covers on the hills – down into Durweston village, where he was killed in a pigsty at Mr Godwin's Brewery. It had been a five-mile run.

'What do you think of the scratch pack now?' Lord Portman asked veteran hunter Henry Symonds. The answer must have been suitably affirmative, as he was invited back to Bryanston House for a first-rate luncheon.

SHORT RUN, EVENTUALLY, FROM SHILLINGSTONE TO STEPLETON HOUSE

Lord Portman's Hounds met in Broadley Wood, above Fairmile on their home estate at Bryanston, on 7 February 1859. They found in Field Grove and went away towards Shillingstone, through Bonsley Common, but then went sideways and from side to side in the valleys of Elcombe and Escombe. At last he descended to the Shillingstone-Blandford turnpike and crossed the meadows and then the River Stour, opposite Hanford House. On the other side he turned south-east, up and over Hod Hill, to drop down to Stepleton House – sometime home of Peter Beckford – and turn north-west, for Child Okeford, but was pulled in Coombe Bottom at Shroton.

The day's invitees, who went back to Bryanston House for lunch, included the Fookes, Burgess and House family contingents, plus the grand old man of Dorset hunting, Henry Symonds.

TURNING FOX DISAPPEARS ON WOOD'S DOWN

Meeting at Winterborne Houghton, Lord Portman's Hounds found in Park Wood on 18 February 1859. The fox broke away over the wall into Delcombe Bottom, heading south-west up and over the hill, then crossed to the other side of Hilton valley, going up through the long plantation to the Ansty road, to Bingham's Melcombe and straight ahead to Henning Hill. Here he turned to the south-east, and ran in the open straight on and over the Devil's Brook to Dewlish Mill and up a drove-way into Wood's Down.

The hounds lost him here in an extraordinary manner, after a quick four miles, in an old trackway. There were some very deep wheel-ruts. Much casting, all around, proved useless. It was presumed that the fox had turned very short and that the hounds had then over-run the scent.

FAMOUS HARLEY GAP RUN OF SIXTEEN MILES IN 72 MINUTES

The season after the death of the first Viscount Portman, who was succeeded by William Henry Berkeley (1829–1919) in 1888, saw the best ever run of the Portman Hunt. They met on 16 January 1890, a crisp day with thin mid-winter sunshine, at Harley Gap, on Ackling Dyke Roman road, above Gussage All Saints. Punctually, huntsman Joe Moss and his two whips brought the splendid dog pack along the down, as the second Viscount and three of his sons rode into view.

The order was given to draw the brake beside the road and then the Atkins family's wood on Manor Farm. Word came that a fox was moving and it duly broke out from the lower end and made northwards for Lord Shaftesbury's Harley Wood. Then he turned east, across Wyke Farm, to Monkton Up Wimborne, where the pack came to a check in the road. Moss held them down-wind towards Wimborne St Giles but finding them uninterested in that, cast them by the meadows to the bridge. Here they were back on his line.

Claimed as one of the fastest runs on record, they took off over open country with hardly a fence, eastwards to Water Lake, Cranborne Farm, and the gap in Bokerley Ditch on Blagdon Hill. Now they were in Hampshire, on Martin Down, but a man was holloaing from Martin Wood. Here, Moss showed his judgment, and let the hounds alone. They pushed on to High Bowlesbury, farms at Ridley, and Allingford Water, to Rockbourne Knoll.

The hounds came out of the gorse as their fox crossed Down Farm for Tennantry Down. He was pulled down just before reaching New Buildings. The hounds had run 16 miles in 72 minutes. The noble master and his sons were at the finish, with Sir Richard Glyn and Admiral Murray, and nearly a dozen ladies were amongst the others close up. They included Mrs Harkness, Miss Munro and Mrs and Miss Parke.

'An Old Master' was the caption to this Spy cartoon of the
2nd Viscount Portman, who continued the Portman
Hunt after his father's death in 1888.

Hounds to the fore and carriages on the drive, with Crichel House being
the stylish setting for a meet of the Portman Hunt, circa 1890.

Chapter Eight

CHARBOROUGH HOUNDS

MR DRAX AND HIS CHARBOROUGH PACK

 The Charborough Hounds of squire John Samuel Wanley Sawbridge Erle Drax M.P. (1800–87) of Charborough Park, Morden, were established in 1833 and hunted all of the Isle of Purbeck, plus an expanse of his own chalkland estate inland to the River Stour. Their territory would expand into Blackmore Vale country after buying hounds from Mr Portman, in 1840, and with Drax moving to his second home, Holnest Park, on the death of his wife – the former Miss Jane Erle-Drax-Grosvenor – in 1853.

Squire Drax hunted wearing a sky-blue coat, cream coloured waistcoat embroidered with gold and a top-hat. His servants, including huntsman John Galton, wore canary-coloured plush coats, with blue collars bound with gold lace, and a gold fox with silver brush on each side of the collar. Their red waistcoats contrasted with white breeches, white tops, black velvet caps and white gloves. Members of the hunt sported scarlet. Sometimes Squire Drax would have everyone mounted on grey horses.

He kept buffalo, trained his dogs to hunt for truffles, and experimented with the re-introduction of wild boar. These were introduced into an area of paled woodland in Charborough Park, beside which he built a parkland pagoda, this being destroyed by lightning in 1838 and replaced by the 120-feet Charborough Tower in 1839.

The Russian breed of boar were found to be more ferocious than the French. Their descendants were eventually removed to Morden. Mr Drax wrote to a friend that he used to shoot them: 'The latter part of the time I kept them at Morden Park, and bred a lot of them, feeding them on turnips and corn. They were savage and troublesome, however, to keep within bounds, and I therefore killed them. They were good eating when fed upon corn.'

The 57-and-a-half couple of the Charborough Hounds, in 1833, were as follows (with 'l' for the ladies):

Seven-years-old – Malcolm.

Six-years-old – Monarch, Saladin, Ruby (l) and Blissful (l).

Five-years-old – Waverley, Marplot, Regent, Rector, Tragedy, Nelson and Magic (l).

Four-years-old – Susan (l), Lunatic, Pugilist, Carver, Reveller, Wonder (l), Pleasant (l), Rakish (l), Grayling (l), Ringlet (l), Richmond, Chaser, Clasper, Cheerful, Foljambe, Torment (l), Lucy (l), Fanny (l), Fancy (l), Constant (l), Milliner (l), Beaufort, Painter, Mospey (l), Manfred, Monarch, Dowager (l), Abelard, Barrister, Lightning (l) and Gossip (l).

Three-years-old – Rosebud (l), Novice (l), Notice, Vaulter, Dorcas (l), Manager, Florist (l), Mindful (l), Ranter, Workman, Selim, Stripling, Warlike, Lofty, Sampson, Roman, Amethyst (l), Jessamine (l), Gratitude (l), Delicate (l), Dorimont, Guardian, Beauty (l), Jingle, Chanter and Dandy.

Two-years-old – Vanity, Jordan (l), Ardent (l), Agatha (l), Palafox, Crafty, Caliban, Scornful (l), Jupiter, Boxer, Verity (l), Favourite (l), Jewess (l), Joyful (l), Warrior, Warderer, Hazard, Restless, Brilliant, Trusty (l) and Boniface.

One-year-old – Famous (l), Precious (l), Portia (l), Priestess (l), Tidings (l), Lovely (l), Charity (l), Welcome (l), Painter, Farmer, Jasper, Larkspur, Telamond, Possum, Blueman, Waverer, Conqueror, Lawless, Bishop, Craftsman, Trinket, Doctor, Wildair, Wildman and Tuneful.

JUST A COUPLE OF MR DRAX'S HOUNDS PERSEVERE WITH THEIR QUARRY

On 28 December 1838 Mr Drax found his fox in a piece of his own gorse on Bere Down, north of Bere Regis, and the hounds went away at a rattling pace to Winterborne Whitechurch and Milton Park. Here, in a cover of 500 acres, they stuck to him for 30 minutes, and got well away down the valley to Whatcombe.

Here the majority of the hounds changed to a fresh fox but a couple of steady hounds persevered and went on to kill the hunted one, after a good run of 75 minutes, without a check.

CHARBOROUGH LADY PACK GO EIGHT MILES AN HOUR, TO FINISH IN MELCOMBE PARK

A large field met Mr Drax at Milborne Wood, Milborne St Andrew, by permission of Mr Farquharson, on 31 December 1838. They drew blank but an old dog fox was found in the gorse on Coles Farm and went away through Milborne Wood, and on to Dewlish.

He then raced away over the wild Druce and Cheselbourne Downs, to Lyscombe, where he skirted the hill into Melcombe Park. The lady pack got up to him, and wished him a Happy New Year, after a brilliant burst of 55 minutes, across an almost straight eight miles, without a check.

FAIR DAY RUN, FROM MILBORNE WOOD TO CHARMINSTER

Another meet of the Charborough Hounds took place at Milborne Wood on 30 November 1840, to coincide with Milborne Fair Day, again by courtesy of Mr Farquharson. They found a fox and went away to the west, to Dewlish House and then south-west through Bason Hill Plantation, on to Druce. Having gone through the west-end hedgerows of the Piddle meadows to Lower Waterston, the fox crossed the road, over Waterston Ridge, south to Grey's Wood and then south-west to Coker's Frome Farm, in sight of Dorchester Prison. Here the hounds turned northwards for their final two miles, up through Higher Burton Farm to Wolfeton Clump, where they killed in Charminster parish. It was a run of ten miles.

FAST RUN FROM ROKE, VIA A NET, TO BHOMPSTON

The Charborough Hounds met on Drax Estate lands at Roke Farm, Bere Regis, on 13 November 1841. John Last was the huntsman and Harry Honey and Jem Penny were the whips. They were all mounted on grey horses, mostly half-bred Arabs, and found in Roke Brake. Having broken away to the south-west, by Roger's Hill Farm, over the meadow and Bere road, they crossed the open Briantspuddle Fields into boggy meadows, leaving the village to the west, and went off south-westwards over the heath, almost to Oakers Wood, where he turned to the west and crossed the Moreton road. Affpuddle Marlpits were left to the south as he headed into Sares Wood.

Here there was a party of rabbiters and the fox went into the long run but managed to escape into Southover Heath, and left Tincleton Hanging to the south. He then went down the hill beside Little Admiston, into the water-meadows of the Frome Valley, and kept the river to the south as he passed Norris Mill and turned north to Duddle Heath and Rainbarrows, and then south-westwards down to the meadows at Bhompston Farm. Here the fox dropped into an open drain, to lie down, and the hounds ran over him.

This time, however, his luck was out. The hounds made their own cast and came back. Their fox jumped up in the middle of them and they pulled him down. It had been a fast run of ten miles.

A FAST EIGHT MILES, FROM GREAT COLL WOOD TO TOLPUDDLE BALL

Great Coll Wood, in the midst of empty chalklands on the northern side of the Drax Estate, provided the setting for the meet of the Charborough Hounds on 3 February 1842. They went away through Little Coll Wood and south across Muston Down, Whitechurch Plantation, and straight ahead over the meadows to Warren's Close and Horse Close, then west over Bere Down to Haywards Farm.

Here they turned south-east, to Roke Farm, and then south-west over the down to West Roke, from where their fox sunk into the valley to cross the water-meadows to Roger's Hill. Here he was pulled down below Tolpuddle Ball.

It had been a fast run of eight miles, followed by a good field, with the hounds in tip-top condition and doing the work mainly by themselves. Charborough Hounds were always well managed and brought straight-necked foxes to hand.

QUICK SEVEN MILES, FROM ROKE TO CHESELBOURNE

On 6 February 1842 the Charborough Hounds met at Roke Brake, in the downs north-west of Bere Regis, and went over Roke Farm to Milborne Farms to the obelisk on Milborne Rings (Weatherby Castle). They crossed the meadows to Warren Farm and then headed north to Milborne Eweleaze and straight through Milborne Big Wood, as it was in those days. The onward course was south-westwards, through Dennet's Bottom, to Crawthorne Farm.

Here the fox turned north, to run the length of the long plantation behind Dewlish House, from one end to the other, and emerged to cross the Milborne-Dewlish road in the direction of West Bagber Copse, which was left to the east. He turned down across Wood's Down and crossed the Devil's Brook, westwards to ascend the hill opposite. Thomas House and his horse had a good ducking! Meanwhile, time and energy were running out for the fox, and he was killed in the middle of Edward Davis' farm at Cheselbourne. It had been another quick chase of seven miles. As James Burgess, of Tarrant Launceston, used to say: 'What very pretty pastime.'

Charborough country, hunted by Squire Drax, included the whole of the Isle of Purbeck and
extended eastwards across what was fast becoming the Victorian new town of Bournemouth.

A rare and interesting shot of beagles in Charborough country in the 1860s,
with tweed and corduroy clad hunt staff, at Creech Grange in the Purbeck Hills.

Chapter Nine

MR RADCLYFFE'S HOUNDS

MR RADCLYFFE'S KENNELS AT HYDE

 Charles James Radclyffe of Hyde House, beside the River Piddle in the heathlands between Bere Regis and Wareham, established an independent kennels and kept his own pack of harriers. Initially, he fell foul of the sensitivities of the county's other huntsmen, and for a time had to content himself with deer, before the final season of Mr Farquharson's Hounds released big blocks of fox country in 1858.

CAYLES DOWN ROEBUCK CHASED TO HIGHER HILTON

Mr Radclyffe's Hounds met at Bagber Farm, north of Milborne St Andrew, on 25 March 1856, and sought to find a black roebuck which had been laying in Cayles Down Coppice during the previous autumn. It was supposed to have escaped from a gentleman's deer park.

Soon they had found it, and were away northwards over Hewish Farm and Luccombe, by Milton Mill, and westwards over the Milborne road to the higher part of Long Ash Farm and Long Close Farm to Coombe Bottom and Bingham's Melcombe. Passing Hilton and Ansty Down he then turned into the valley at Higher Hilton and was killed in the farmyard. He was very fat and could not stand a long run being in sight of the hounds for the whole four miles.

HUNTED DEER SURVIVES DEWLISH PARK SHOTGUN BUT NOT FOR LONG

Meeting at Tolpuddle village, on 6 April 1856, Mr Radclyffe's Hounds headed northwards to have a drag from Lord's Down to Milborne Wood. A fine old roebuck had taken up quarters there for several seasons. Mr Radclyffe was aware that Mr Farquharson was jealous of anyone keeping harriers, or interfering with his covers, and felt uncomfortable on such hallowed ground.

Charles Davis saw the deer jump up in the Dewlish corner of the wood. He was away at once, over Cole's Farm, to the valley at Bagber, and north to Hewish Farm and Wood's Down. He stopped for a 'refresher' while crossing the brook. He then headed south-west, over Tuck's Farm, and then Chebbard Farm, where he turned south-east and entered Dewlish Park.

The chase nearly stopped here, as a gentleman shot both barrels at him – unaware he was being hunted – but without any effect. By now he was back on home territory, heading through the long plantation and back into Milborne Wood, but he went out again. This time he went across Mr Kent's farm, left Dewlish parish to the south, and crossed the large fields for Cheselbourne village where he was pulled down under the clump of pines on Tuck's Down.

ROEBUCK RUN FROM WHITECHURCH TO MORDEN PARK CORNER

Having met at Whitechurch Plantation, Winterborne Whitechurch, on 13 April 1856, Mr Radclyffe's Hounds found an old buck, which went straight away down over Muston Farm and Abbot's Court Farm to cross the Kingston road and Besant's Farm. Then he crossed the Wimborne-Bere turnpike to Bloxworth Farm, leaving Bere Wood to the west, to run the Bloxworth covers. He was killed in Morden mill-pond, near Morden Park Corner.

STICKLAND VILLAGERS CAPTURE AND SKIN A LYTCHETT BUCK

Meeting in Lytchett High Wood, to hunt a one-horn buck which had escaped from Charborough Park, Mr Radclyffe's Hounds chased it back towards the parkland. He made two attempts at the high wall near Lion Lodge and succeeded in crossing it. Then he skirted the deer park, going over the open fields, through Westley Woods and passing Almer Woods. From here he went north-westwards, across Spetisbury Farm and Starve-all Farm, to Great Coll Wood. He proceeded to cross the expanse of downs, and then the Blandford-Dorchester turnpike, over Thornicombe Farm, to the top part of the Down House plantations.

Here he turned westwards, over to Clenston and Quarleston, and then north up the valley into Winterborne Stickland village. The hounds were a long way behind, having covered eleven miles, and also had a long check. By the time they reached Stickland they found that the buck, which ran into an outhouse, had not only had his throat cut but was strung up and being skinned. There was a rumpus between Mr Radclyffe and the men but they gave up the deer in exchange for a little silver for drinks, which put matters on a friendly footing.

INCREDIBLE RUN OF TWENTY-FIVE MILES ENDS UNDER JULIAN'S BRIDGE AT WIMBORNE

The best run that Mr Radclyffe's Hounds ever achieved, and probably the best of its kind in Dorset, was from Lytchett High Wood, on 3 April 1857. It lasted 250 minutes in continuous rain to reach an incredible distance of 25 miles. An old roebuck broke away for Lytchett Manor House, through the covers, and over the road from Bailey Gate to Poole, into Henbury plantations. He then turned eastwards over that enormous expanse of wild heath nearly to the railway lines of Poole Junction at Hamworthy, where he turned short and went back all through the Henbury covers again.

Then he crossed the Blandford-Wimborne turnpike, crossing the meadows and a swollen River Stour at White Mill – a much-needed refresher for all concerned – eastwards towards Badbury Rings. He turned south from the ancient entrenchments, over the downs and the old Blandford-Wimborne turnpike, to Kingston Lacy House. Once more he was in the meadows, hiding for some time in a large spear-bed, and then jumped up in full view and swam the Stour again.

This gave him fresh life and he followed the south bank for two miles, into Wimborne, where he took refuge under Julian's Bridge, beneath the arch closest to the bank, with his fine head and antlers just out of the water. He was soon ousted and killed.

The horses were thoroughly exhausted. Charles Parke invited the horsemen back to Henbury House, with the horses being first to eat and drink, and Mr Parke received them in the dining room: 'Have a good glass of this old rum; it will warm you up. I believe it has been in this house nearly a hundred years.'

BAGGED FOX RUNS HOME TO ASHLEY CHASE

On 5 December 1858, after the final season of Mr Farquharson's Hounds, Mr Radclyffe's pack were invited to Bradford Plantations, Bradford Peverell, as no one would be hunting foxes in the Cattistock country, until Lord Poltimore took it over in 1859. They soon found and went southward, across the Dorchester-Bridport turnpike, to Martinstown and the Hardy Monument (erected in 1845 as a memorial to Nelson's flag-captain at Trafalgar), where they turned, over Steepleton Cowleaze and the Abbotsbury-Dorchester road, to Bridehead Farmhouse. On the hill opposite, after the big eweleazes, they left the old trackway to Portesham and Gorwell to the south, to Foxholes Coppice and went westwards to the water-meadows of Lower Kingston Russell and on to Long Bredy, which was a few fields to the north, as they crossed stiff fences to reach the Litton Cheney road.

The chase then turned southwards, through Nine Acres cover and Ashley Woods to Look Wood and Puncknowle Wood, where everyone was obliged to stop with darkness closing in. It soon became common knowledge that this fox had run nine miles to return home. For he had been caught in a rabbit net in Ashley Woods the previous day and was carried by a gentleman, in a bag in his carriage, to Bradford where he was turned out as the hounds met there in the morning. The field's homeward tracks were to the King's Arms in Dorchester where they rested themselves and their horses.

SHILVINGHAMPTON CIRCUIT ENDS ON CORTON HILL

A week later, on 13 December 1858, Mr Radclyffe's Hounds met at Buckland Wood, Buckland Ripers, near Chickerell. Foxes were scarce in the Weymouth hinterland, because they were no longer tolerated as a result of Mr Farquharson retiring from the sport, and it was three hours of drawing before they at last found in a furze-brake at Shilvinghampton.

They went away south-westwards to Wyke Wood and turned short to the east, over the somewhat tricky brook towards Rodden Ridge, and then turned again for Langton Herring and the Fleet coast. Instead, however, this short-running and twisting fox changed direction again and headed for the hills. The pack went through Buckland Wood, Dairyhouse Coppice, and over the vale claylands to Friar Waddon Eweleazes on the limestone ridge. The fox then headed south-westwards for the Corton Gap, to sink back into familiar flatlands, but this was its last burst and he was killed on the side of Corton Hill. He had run five miles to return to within a mile of home.

BERE FOX CIRCLES THE DOWNS AND THEN RUNS FOR MORDEN BOG

Meeting in their home parish, at Piddle Wood on the slope above Shitterton, Bere Regis, Mr Radclyffe's Hounds found an old stager in Spring Gardens on 8 January 1859. They broke away to the south-west, over the Briantspuddle fields, and turned north across Roger's Hill meadows and farm, to Roke Down. Crossing the Bere-Milborne road, over Haywards Farm, he went across Bere Down and Whitechurch Farm, then into Horse Close Plantation, where the pack had their first check.

In five minutes they were off again, to Kingston Farm and over the hill at the clump of firs on Muddox Barrow. He then went south-east, over the covers of Bloxworth Down, to complete a straight two miles at the Cock and Bottle in East Morden (a favourite meet of Mr Drax's Hounds). Here he turned south, across the Bere-Poole road, and was killed near Mr Young's farmhouse in Morden Bog. A large field followed this brilliant ten-mile run, including Lord Poltimore on his chestnut horse, The Cardinal.

From Morden Park to the Town Walls at Wareham

Mr Radclyffe's Hounds were back in Morden Park on 1 February 1859, having met on Bloxworth Green. They broke away for Morden Mill, through the Bloxworth covers and into the corner of Bere Wood. Then they re-crossed the Bere-Poole road, southwards across the heath to Pickard's Lookout (Woolsbarrow) where he tried the earths but found them stopped.

So he turned south-west, across the Bere-Wareham road, to the long bog below Sugar Hill, and on through the plantation to the home ground for the pack at Hyde House. Heading down the Piddle meadows, south-eastwards to Binnegar Mill, he then crossed the river and went south over the heath to Holme Bridge, where he crossed the road and went on to the River Frome. This he did not cross. Instead he turned to the east, following the river down to Worgret House. Here he turned north-east, crossing the road by the old entrenchments, heading for Wareham where he would be killed on the Town Walls at Bloody Bank.

Hiding fox bagged and returned to Milborne after run of thirteen miles

Meeting at Winterborne Whitechurch on 16 March 1863, Mr Radclyffe's Hounds drew Horse Close Plantation, south of the village, and then found a fox in a chalkpit on Kingston Farm. He went straight over Bere Down to Haywards Farm and then south-westwards across Milborne Down, leaving Foxpound to the north. He crossed Milborne Rings (Weatherby Castle) and went over the meadows to Warren Hill where William Henry Berkeley (1829–1919, second Viscount Portman) and Henry Symonds viewed him two fields ahead.

Following breast-high scent the hounds crossed the corn-fields on Mr Homer's farm and Tolpuddle Eweleaze to Burleston Hill and on across the water-meadows. Colonel Napier Sturt and Captain Quick were amongst those who took the opportunity for a cold bath in the brook.

The pace was also beginning to take its toll. The pack had a long check on the top of Bason Hill, at the crossroads on the Puddletown-Blandford turnpike, in order to ease the horses. Reynard must have been a couple of miles ahead when huntsman George Kennett cast down the hollow trackway, and the hounds hit it over the Dewlish road to Paul's Farm and over into the Druce hedgerows. They kept on straight over Druce Eweleaze and across the Muston meadows to Barn Coppice. Here there was poor scent across two miles of ploughed land to Dole's Ash, which lay a little to the east, as they continued northwards to cross the road from Piddletrenthide to Plush. Also passing to the east of Plush and Whatcombe Wood he dropped down into the Blackmore Vale through the centre of Armswell big cover, to Alton Common, before the building of the dairy-house and its large yard. Here Mr Radclyffe, with Symonds and Kennett, saw their fox – dead-beat after 13 miles – going round the corner of a hay-rick beside the yard gates. All the cow-stalls, pigsties and outhouses were tried. Mr Radclyffe eventually ordered the hounds home after Kennett's best run after a fox.

En route to hospitality with Michael Miller, Symonds and his companions reached the Fox Inn at Plush (where the hostelry is now the Brace of Pheasants). A man on horseback caught them up to say that the fox had been found in a closet and was now in a bag. Mr Miller had him brought to Plush and let loose for the night in safe keeping. Mr Radclyffe asked for him to be brought back and turned loose in Milborne furze-brake for another day's sport.

While he was in captivity, Symonds made an inch-long slit in each ear and cut off their tips, in order to recognise him again. That day would come in 1866, when he was found in Admiston willow-bed and ran for 40 minutes over Tolpuddle, Roger's Hill, Roke, and turned back south of Milborne St Andrew, westwards to Warren Hill. He was pulled down on Lord's Down, opposite the old Dewlish Turnpike Gate, at the Crawthorne junction.

EIGHT-MILE RUN, FROM DRUCE TO MAPPOWDER

Mr Radclyffe's Hounds met at Druce House on 13 January 1864 and drew the hedgerows and Hill's Coppice blank. Joined by Lord Poltimore, they found in a noted pit in a large corn-field called Wiltshire Walls and went away with a good scent over Furzey Down, straight through Dole's Hill Plantation, Dole's Ash Hogleazes, and the big eweleazes to Lyscombe Hill. Leaving Plush to the west, they continued northwards down the great escarpment at Nettlecombe Tout, on through Spring's Coppice to Monkwood Hill, leaving Melcombe Park to the east.

Having crossed the brook they killed at the crossroads close to Mappowder House, where the James family had lived for so many years, and bred prize-winning Hereford cattle. It had been an eight-mile run.

HOUNDS DO IT THEMSELVES, FROM HETHFELTON TO ADMISTON

Meeting at home, at Hyde House, on 27 January 1864, Mr Radclyffe's Hounds drew Stoke Heath blank and went southwards into Hethfelton Plantation, where the hounds found a fox and went off by themselves at a racing pace north-westwards over the heath and Bovington Bog to Moreton Plantation and North Lodge (since demolished), beside the Dorchester-Wareham road on the west side of Clouds Hill. From here there was a view of the hounds going out of Oakers Wood, over the heath to Waddock Drove and into Marlpits Wood. Leaving Sares Wood to the north they continued westwards across Pallington Heath, all through the cover called Tincleton Hangings, and he was pulled down without a check after eight miles, at Little Admiston.

The hounds had it all to themselves, well ahead of the field, across the most difficult heath and bog country. It was crossed by many blind wheel-ruts concealed by long heather. As a result there were many bad falls as horse and rider went heels over head.

ANOTHER SEVEN MILES, FROM HETHFELTON TO AFFPUDDLE

Another outing with Mr Radclyffe's Hounds from close to home, having met at Worgret willow-bed on 8 February 1864, also trotted on to Hethfelton. Jem Treadwell joined them for the day, and cheered on the hounds, when he could get near them.

They found in that dependable wilderness and went away northwards for Hyde before turning north-west for Gallows Hill and Chamberlayne's Heath, to Harry Little's Clump. Finding the big earths there all stopped, the fox turned short to the right and followed the long bog to Cecily Bridge over the River Piddle. He ran down the south side of the river to Throop and Briantspuddle and then crossed the river, to put his head northwards for Piddle Wood, which he did not reach. He was pulled down, after seven miles, in the open fields at Affpuddle.

GENTRY OUT IN FORCE AS SIX-MILER ESCAPES, FROM PLUSH TO BAKER'S FOLLY

There was a gentrified field following Mr Radclyffe's Hounds when they met at Kingrove, Piddletrenthide, on 1 March 1864. They included Mr and Mrs Hambro (the latter riding high Chaldon) from Milton Abbey. Monty Guest from Canford House, the Provincial Grand Master for Dorsetshire, was present with Joseph Pearkes Fox Gundry from Bridport. Miss Manley attended from Dorchester (her father kept the King's Arms). Mr Gundry lost his hat at the start, but would not stop to dismount, and rode the run bare-headed.

There was nothing to run after in the morning but in the afternoon, at Plush, they found in Watcombe Bottom and headed north-east, through Armswell, and took to the Blackmore Vale at Spring's Coppice. They went on to Monkwood Hill and Humber Wood. Crossing the stiff enclosures and brook, to Stoke Common, this stout fox was returning to his home hills.

He went westwards up and over Bulbarrow and then straight ahead, between Woolland rabbit warren and Delcombe Head, with the hounds racing for blood. Just as the six-mile run was expected to reach its conclusion, however, they had a check on the side of the escarpment, near Baker's Folly. They cast for Ibberton Park and Houghton Stubbs but to no avail.

HENRY SYMONDS RELEASES A BAGGED FOX ON ROGER'S HILL

Mr Radclyffe's Hounds met at Milborne Wood on 7 March 1864. In case they did not find, Henry Symonds, in his old wood-shed at Milborne St Andrew, had an old dog fox which had been sent over by Michael Miller, from Plush, having been dug out at Armswell the day before. They not only drew the wood but moved on to Tolpuddle Eweleaze, Tolpuddle Common, and Warren Hill.

Symonds asked retired huntsman Jem Treadwell to go back to Milborne and bring the fox in a bag. He released him in a piece of high rape on Roger's Hill Farm and remained out of sight until George Kennett, the huntsman, appeared with the hounds. They found his line into Milborne Rings (Weatherby Castle), where he was dodging about, and forced his departure eastwards to Roke Brakes, and then south over the Bere Stream water-meadows to Piddle Wood and Spring Gardens, and down to the water-meadows of the River Piddle at Throop Farm. Here Mr Walden – riding a chestnut mare – cleared a distance of 33 feet, out of a halter-path and over a hedge and brook, to land in a meadow. Several of the field, after the run was over, went back and measured it.

Gerard Sturt (later Lord Alington) tried to get over the boggy meadows, but failed, and had to retrace into a road, via Briantspuddle. The hounds went on southwards, at a burning scent across the heath, and crossed the long bog between the Dead Woman's Stone (since removed) and North Lodge (demolished) to cross the road from Waddock Cross to Gallows Hill and skirt Clouds Hill as he escaped towards Bovington. He had gone six miles. His origin, ten miles away in the opposite direction, remained a secret between Treadwell and Symonds. The rest of the field thought they were following a genuine fox.

SECRET 'BAG-MAN' RUNS FROM MILBORNE RINGS TO MUSTON DOWN

Bagged foxes were becoming something of a specialty for Henry Symonds, who received another in time for the meet of Mr Radclyffe's Hounds at Roke Down, Bere Regis, on 19 March 1864. They drew Foxpound blank and the brought fox was let out of a bag just as the hounds began to draw the next cover to the west, at Milborne Rings (Weatherby Castle).

Charlie soon took the hint and was off like a shot over Milborne Farm, Stanfield's Fields, and across the Blandford-Dorchester turnpike, northwards over Deverel Farm and Bagber Farm, to Hewish and Luccombe Cottages.

Here he turned east, through the lower part of Milton Park, and left Whatcombe House to the south. Then, after crossing Whatcombe Farm, he was seen crossing the fields for Whitechurch Plantation, which he had just strength enough to struggle through, into Muston Down where the hounds pulled him down, without a single check, after seven miles. Again the field was unaware that this was a 'bag-man'. Symonds knew that these old foxes generally run well, if they are not kept more than a few hours after being dug out, and are then released in a different part of the country.

YELLOWHAM RUN ENDS AT CERNE ABBAS

Meeting in Yellowham Wood, on 5 April 1864, Mr Radclyffe's Hounds soon found and went away through Grey's Wood, into the chalklands at Waterston Ridge, and continued north-west to Wolfeton Clump, Burton Farm, and Lord Ilchester's brake. He turned north into the broad downlands between the Cerne and Piddle valleys, to Holcombe and Kingrove. From there he headed west, over the Old Sherborne Road, to Well Bottom and the side of Black Hill, above the meadows beside Cerne town, where they pulled him down.

The scent was high and strong so the hounds had it all to themselves. It was an excellent ten-mile ride across open country.

RARE TRAVELLER DOES A COMPLETE CIRCUIT TO SAFETY AT ADMISTON

Mr Radclyffe's Hounds met at Druce House on 12 April 1864 and had a frustrating morning in the hedgerows around Bush Coppice. In the afternoon they were down the valley on the other side of Puddletown, drawing Admiston willow-bed and Mr Crane's cover. These were also blank but a rare traveller was lying in the spinney by Mr Homer's house at Tolpuddle.

He broke away northwards over Tolpuddle Farm, Warren Hill, Milborne Eweleaze and Milborne Wood. Then he turned westwards, over Crawthorne Farm, and crossed the Dewlish water-meadows and cowleazes to Bason Hill. There he turned southwards, to head home down the valley to Admiston Farm, and over the brook and meadows to Mr Brymer's house at Ilsington. Having crossed the Dorchester-Bere turnpike beside Athelhampton parish church, he went through Mr Homer's coppice, into Cowpound Wood. Here he saved his brush by getting into the main earth just ahead of the hounds. They had run five miles without a check.

SHORT WOOD RUN ENDS WITH ESCAPE INTO DRAIN FOR BUTTERWICK JACK

Henry Symonds junior, riding one of his father's horses, Oxford (bought from Simmonds of Oxford, by Charles Radclyffe), joined the meet of Mr Radclyffe's Hounds on 12 November 1865. They found in Short Wood, Mappowder, and went off after a good scent north to Humber Wood, and then west across the River Lydden at Cannings Court. They crossed the road between the Halsey Arms and the Green Man to Ponting's Gorse and the stiff fences to Holwell Plantation. Here he turned to Buckshaw House, where that noted rider Mr Littleshales lived so many years, and through Buckshaw Brake.

Continuing westwards, crossing Caundle Marsh brook, he passed to the north of Folke and approached that famous cover called Butterwick Wood. In a field close by he entered a long drain after a run of six miles. As there was no chance of bolting him, Mr Radclyffe ordered the hounds back to Hyde, on the other side of the county.

Old timers recalled that Ben Jennings always used to say there were foxes which the hounds would never kill. The Blackmore Vale had a brace. One was known as Butterwick Jack and the other Short Wood Hector. Their counterpart on Cranborne Chase was Chetterwood Jack.

The two legendary 15-mile chases with the latter were from a Crichel Park meet to Duncliffe Hill – where they were to meet the following day – when they duly followed him home. Billy Butler used to wish them all a natural death in advanced old age.

It was after this meeting with Butterwick Jack that the ramifications of Mr Wingfield Digby buying the Mappowder property caused Short Wood and Humber Wood to be handed over to the Blackmore Vale Hunt. This was regarded as a great loss by Symonds and Radclyffe and all their friends from the South.

DASH FROM DEVIL'S BROOK ENDS WITH SAVED BRUSH UNDER WOODBURY HILL

Having met at Bingham's Melcombe on 26 November 1865, and failed to find on Henning Hill, Mr Radclyffe's Hounds gradually worked their way southwards to Cheselbourne and then east across the Devil's Brook. Here they found an old stager, in a high piece of rape on George Groves' farm, near West Bagber Copse. He went away to Groves' barn, south-eastwards towards Bagber Farm, and crossed the Milborne-Milton Abbas road near Deverel Farm. Then he made for Longthorns, crossed the Blandford-Puddletown turnpike, and dashed for Whitechurch Farm.

He went straight through Horse Close and over Kingston Down, through the fir clump on top to Muddox Barrow. Crossing the Bere-Wimborne road he just touched the south corner of Bere Wood and saved his brush by going into the big earth under Woodbury Hill. It had been a very quick thing, across six miles, with an almost perfect scent and no check throughout.

GRAND WHO-WHOOP AFTER TEN-MILE CIRCUIT OF FOSSIL FARM

Meeting at Warmwell sheep-wash on 3 December 1865, Mr Radclyffe's Hounds found in the long bog on Galton Heath and broke away southwards over Galton Common to Fossil Farm. Crossing the Dorchester-Wool turnpike and the big arable fields he made for the High Chaldon earths – which were closed – and then over open downland, up and down those trying hills, to Holworth and on to the top of the cliffs, above Ringstead Bay, for two miles.

He turned east to Upton Farm and went into the plantations beside Poxwell House and then turned northwards over the eweleazes into Watercombe Farm. Here he turned east, to complete his circuit, across Owermoigne Farm and over the road at Fossil Farm, to be killed in a small willow-bed close to Winfrith Newburgh parish. It was a severe and trying run of ten miles, both for hounds and horses, and there was a grand who-whoop.

ONE ALL AFTER DOUBLE CIRCUITS, MORNING AND AFTERNOON

The meet of Mr Radclyffe's Hounds on 10 December 1865, at Piddlehinton Cross, spent the morning chasing a ringing fox around Piddletrenthide and Giant's Head. Having killed near Cerne Abbas they were drawing on homewards when a fox jumped out of a chalkpit on Lovelace's Farm, Piddlehinton, and went away close to his brush, to Dole's Hill and over Druce Down. He then crossed Chebbard Farm and Dewlish Warren to Bason Hill, where he turned sharply to the west.

Returning to his home landscape, via Paul's Farm and Druce Down, he followed the hedgerows on Muston Eweleaze, passing Burn Coppice, and went to ground in the deep rabbit earth close to Muston farmhouse. It had been a run of nine miles that ended almost where it started.

NINE-MILE ESCAPE, FROM CAME HOUSE TO FRIAR WADDON

Mr Radclyffe's Hounds met at Came House on 6 March 1866 and found in a furze-brake close by, and went away up and over Came Farm and through Came Wood, close to Culliford Tree, and headed for Sutton quarries. He then turned west, over the Walls and Bincombe Hill, to Ridgeway Hill railway tunnel and the Dorchester-Weymouth road.

On the other side he crossed the Upwey quarries and turned northwards up Gould's Bottom, crossing the Martinstown road, and going straight ahead over the hills to Winterborne Monkton. Then he turned westwards, across Ashton Farm, and veered south-west up and over Ridge Hill to turn short of Friar Waddon Farm and run along the big eweleazes facing the Buckland Ripers vale. He just saved his brush, after nine miles, by going into the main earths in the side of Waddon Hill.

FROM WEST KNIGHTON TO SAFETY, UNDER THE WHITE HORSE

Meeting at Warmwell sheep-wash on 21 March 1866 and drawing several covers blank, Mr Radclyffe's Hounds found in a West Knighton willow-bed, where foxes like to lie on top of the hassocks. They went away over the heath and straight through Knighton Plantation, then across the open fields, and into the Friarmayne woods.

The chase continued straight ahead over the Broadmayne-Dorchester road, south-westwards for Came Park, but being hard-pressed and with the wind in his teeth, he turned around to cross the West Knighton and Whitcombe Farms in the direction of Culliford Tree. He then sunk the hill, running the whole length of Sutton Farm, where he went to ground in the big earths under the White Horse, the chalk-cut equestrian figure of King George, above Osmington.

TWELVE-MILE CIRCUIT, FROM HARTFOOT LANE TO WOOLLAND

Mr Radclyffe's Hounds met at Henning Hill, Bingham's Melcombe, on 22 October 1873, with huntsman Henry Beviss. They found in Aldermore on the north-west side of Hartfoot Lane and ran on to Fern Wood, where they had a ring in that cover, and broke away on the lower edge, out to the north-east, via Breach Wood to Pleck, Rawlsbury Camp and Lamplings. He then ran westwards to Mappowder and turned there to the north-east, for Hazelbury Bryan and Locketts Farm. Leaving Deadmoor Common to the north he then turned to the south to head back towards his home hills.

By now, however, the pace and distance were telling, and the hounds pulled him down in the middle of the Long Wood at Woolland. The hounds had covered more than twelve miles, in 100 minutes.

THREE VERY DIFFERENT FOXES FOUND IN BEAULIEU WOOD

Meeting at Castle Hill, Duntish, on 6 December 1873, Mr Radclyffe's Hounds went to Beaulieu Wood, by wish of Captain Glyn. A fox was found close by and ran to Short Wood, Mappowder, to earth. Then a second fox was found in Beaulieu Wood and ran north-west to West Pulham and Rabbits Coppice. It then turned south, to Dungeon Hill, and a sharp change of course down into Great Wootton Wood, where it was killed after a fast 35 minutes.

Their third fox was found in Woodfalls and ran by Middlemarsh to Grange Woods, then re-crossed the Sherborne-Dorchester road below Lyon's Gate, to Clinger Farmhouse. He turned over the hill, leaving Mount Silver to the west, down to Little Minterne and around High Cank to Up Cerne Wood. He then headed westwards across the valley for Fernycombe and Red Post. Crossing Eastcombe Bottom to Row Hill, above Up Sydling, he continued westwards, into White's Wood and across Batcombe Hill. Here he went to ground in the main earths by the hillside church, after a run of ten miles in 78 minutes.

FAST THIRTEEN MILES, FROM HIGHER ANSTY TO SOUTH ADMISTON

Meeting at Bingham's Melcombe on 18 December 1873, Mr Radclyffe's Hounds trotted on to Breach Wood, Higher Ansty, and found a fox which broke away to the north-west towards Mappowder. It then turned south, through Cockroad Copse, to pass the western side of Melcombe Park, and went over the hill, through Ball Bottom Copses, to Folly and Lyscombe.

He then turned to the north-east, through Summer-house Copse at Bingham's Melcombe, and then south over the Cheselbourne farms, on to Druce Farm. Passing Mr Hull's house, he crossed the water-meadows to Troy Town and crossed the Dorchester-Puddletown road for the hill and heath to Ilsington Wood. On the other side he was viewed a mile to the north-east, going to ground in the main earth at Cowpound Wood, South Admiston.

Here he was left for another day, in Mr Crane's cover, after a fine and fast run. Thirteen miles were covered in 75 minutes.

GOING ROUND IN CIRCLES ON CHRISTMAS EVE

The Christmas Eve meet of Mr Radclyffe's Hounds in 1873 was at Armswell, between Folly and Mappowder, and they found in Dairyhouse Coppice. It ran to earth in Buckland Knoll, in a rabbit spout, with Levi Sheppard being left to dig it out. Their second fox came from Alton Bottom Copse and went on over the hill through Alton Ivors, to Henley, where it turned to the right over Buckland Knoll. It then went back to Henley, over the hill, and crossed Mr Hawkins' farm.

Then it made for the downs, crossing Giant's Head and Sherry's Tout Gorse, but turned back for the Blackmore Vale and descended through the Clinger Covers and Mount Silver, crossing the Cerne-Sherborne road at Lyon's Gate. It then went westwards along the side of High Stoy to Seat Copse and Hilfield, then southwards to Ruppen Copse to earth.

It was a twisting and circling run, but fine hunting, of 68 minutes. The hounds must have gone seven or eight miles. As a reward the whip, Levi Sheppard, came up with the first fox for them to eat.

RECORD TWELVE MILES IN 55 MINUTES, TO DELCOMBE HEAD

The Boxing Day meet of Mr Radclyffe's Hounds in 1873 was at Horse Close Plantation, on the downs south-west of Winterborne Whitechurch. They drew blank all across Henry Fookes' farm, then likewise in the Reformatory gorse beside Little Wood Industrial School (Longmead), and also West Bagber Copse. Then they moved southwards towards Milborne St Andrew and found.

He gave them a sharp 20 minutes in a circuit of Dewlish and Druce and back around to the lower side of Milborne Wood, from Dennet's Bottom to Betsy Cain's Grave, where he was tallied by William Fookes. Heading north, he skirted West Bagber Copse and went over the farms to the wall at Milton Abbas, through the plantation and across the park, to the far length of wall and Delcombe Head. Here he was pulled down, virtually on Bulbarrow Hill, after as fast a run as there is on record. It covered 12 miles in 55 minutes.

CLINKING THIRTEEN-MILE RUN, GOING TO GROUND IN STOKE WOOD

At a meet at Bingham's Melcombe on 26 March 1874, Mr Radclyffe's Hounds found in Breach Wood and ran a ring of 20 minutes in Fern Wood, where they killed a brace. They disturbed their third fox in Melcombe Park where it turned about in that thick cover before breaking away northwards to Cockroad and Mappowder.

It went on to Short Wood and Humber Wood, with the field following at a good pace, but then turned back to Short Wood and went off westwards this time. Going through Beaulieu, as if for Castle Hill, some schoolboys headed it to Duntish Common. Then it turned east at Cannings Court and went through Humber Wood for the second time – exiting up the

Blackmore Vale to the Mappowder brook – and made for Stoke Mills. It was finally viewed over the hill going to ground in the main earth in Stoke Wood. This was a clinking run of more than 13 miles in 95 minutes.

During the 1873-74 season Mr Radclyffe's Hounds hunted 57 days (including two blank days and one too foggy to ride) and killed 46 adult foxes, plus another 19 cubbing, to make a total of 65. They also ran 23 to ground. It was Mr Radclyffe's rule not to dig but leave them for another day.

THIRTEEN MILES OF CIRCUIT AND RUN, ENDING AT ILSINGTON HOUSE

A decade later, with Levi Sheppard as the huntsman, Mr Radclyffe's Hounds met at Sares Wood, Affpuddle, on 14 December 1883 and found on Tolpuddle Ball. They ran eastwards on to Bere Down and then turned back to Roke and the meadows below Roger's Hill. Having completed a circuit, he then headed south-eastwards for Piddle Wood and the furze-brake on Black Hill, Bere Regis, where the hounds had a long check.

He was then off again, into Spring Gardens, and turned south-west from the boggy meadows at Briantspuddle, crossing the River Piddle and Affpuddle Heath, to Sares Wood. Marlpits Wood, Pallington Heath and Tincleton Hanging were left to the south as he headed west, in a line across Southover Heath, to Fir Mount and Cowpound Wood. Having tried the Admiston covers and Chapel Copse, near Ilsington House, he was pulled down after 14 miles and 70 minutes.

FAST SEVEN MILES, FROM TOLPUDDLE TO MILTON ABBAS

Meeting in Milborne St Andrew village on 8 January 1884, Mr Radclyffe's Hounds drew Milborne Wood, Bason Hill and Admiston willow-bed, with all proving blank. They found eventually, by Tolpuddle Eweleaze, and ran across the open on to Warren Hill and crossed the meadows to Castle Rings (Weatherby Castle), over Milborne Farm to Foxpound, where he turned over Stanfield's Farm and the Blandford-Puddletown turnpike, northwards across Deverel Farm, Bagber Farm and Luccombe Farm.

He was pulled down in the open, above Milton Abbas village, just before reaching the Milton Park Wood. It had been a very fast run of seven miles in 45 minutes.

'AS GAME A FOX AS EVER WAS KILLED' AT THROOP FARM

Mr Radclyffe's Hounds met at Dole's Hill on 16 January 1884, with the fine day encouraging a good muster to turn out, and they soon found a fox. It was ringed around for a short time and killed. Then they drew the hedgerows on William Shetler Hull's farm at Druce, where the landowner was that staunch sportsman William Ernest Brymer M.P., of Ilsington House. A stout customer was found and went off over the water-meadows to Ilsington Heath, where he went to ground.

Their third customer stole away just as the other went to earth. He headed north-west, through Yellowham, to the top of Waterston Ridge, where a shepherd turned him back to Yellowham Wood. He also returned straight ahead over the Dorchester road to Ilsington Heath and the big wood, where he broke away eastwards over the Puddletown-Moreton road across Tincleton fields and Tincleton Hangings. Here he bore on, over Southover Heath and into Sares Wood, then out over the allotments and the road from Affpuddle to Moreton Station. Leaving the Marlpits to the south he went over the top of the heath above Oaker's Wood, and crossed Briantspuddle Brick Works and the road to North Lodge, and ran the other road a mile to beyond Throop Clump.

Here he turned south-east, to cross the long bog and heath, to Chamberlayne's Bridge. He then altered course to run the road again and return to Throop Clump, where he lay down by the roadside, until forced up again by the leading hound. They ran into him in the open, in the middle of a field on Throop Farm, after 13 miles in 145 minutes, without a check. 'He was as game a fox as ever was killed,' Henry Symonds remarked.

There was a shock for Captain Robert Fitzroy, who dropped his whip a moment before, and dismounted to pick it up. His horse then abandoned him and made straight for home.

TWENTY-MILE RUN WINS PRAISE FROM COLONEL HAMBRO

The 15 March 1884 meet of Mr Radclyffe's Hounds was on Black Hill at Bere Regis from where they drew the Piddle Valley westwards to Affpuddle willow-beds and turned north to Tolpuddle Ball and across the chalklands, approaching Horse Close Coppice. All was blank till then, when Mr R. Cave turned a fox and a hare out of a small pit.

The fox went off towards Winterborne Whitechurch, turned to pass south of Longthorns, and then headed north over Chescombe Farm to Milton Park Wood. He turned south-west to Luccombe Hill but was headed, first by a man cracking flints, and then by a flock of sheep, southwards down the valley to Hewish Farm, West Bagber Copse, and Milton Wood. Here he turned around twice, with the pack sticking to him, and left along the Blandford-Dorchester road to the old Dewlish Turnpike Gate.

Here he turned north, along the lane to Crawthorne Farm, where Henry Symonds observed him standing in the middle of a field, listening for hounds to come into view. He then ran another 30 minutes, to Bason Hill, and crossed the Puddletown-Blandford turnpike, heading westwards over Mr Paul's farm, to Druce House. He was then headed back over the large arable fields and their hedgerow, and went for half a mile along the lane towards Dewlish. His final turn was southwards, for Puddletown, and he yielded up his life in the open, by John Domett Paul's house at Lower Waterston.

The time was 185 minutes and the distance 20 miles, though he had been turned so much that it was only half that from point to point. Colonel Charles Joseph Theophilus Hambro M.P., from Milton Abbey, said it was as good a run as he ever saw. Henry Symonds' hunting wisdom was that foxes found in pits invariably made for the best runners.

Eight-mile run ends at Minterne ice-house

The Piddlehinton Cross meet of Mr Radclyffe's Hounds on 26 March 1884 drew blank at Muston and in James Lovelace's brakes on East Farm. They found further north, in Kingrove, above Piddletrenthide, and went up and down across Holcombe and Hadsham and into Eight Acre Coppice, as if for Chandler's Coppice and Castle Hill in the Blackmore Vale. Instead he turned to the west on the spring-line, to Clinger Far, where huntsman Kit Atkinson was pensioned off by Viscount Portman.

He went across the Cerne-Sherborne road at Dogbury Gate and followed the hanging covers of High Stoy, before turning south into Up Cerne Woods, leaving Sydling Clappers to the west. Having passed Up Cerne House and crossed the road again, to Lord Digby's parkland at Minterne Magna, this fox then sought shelter in some ivy on top of the ice-house.

On being dislodged, he fell into the hounds' mouths, to end this eight-mile run.

Vixen crosses the unrideable heath to Morden Park

Owing to an illness in the family, Mr and Mrs Radclyffe missed the meet of their hounds on 13 December 1884 when Levi Sheppard took the 'Beauties' to Great Col Wood on the downs above Mapperton and Almer. It was raining steadily, without any wind, and they soon found a brace of foxes. Settling down to one, which proved to be a vixen, they put a ring around the cover which caused her to break away southwards across the young wheat. She made for Winterborne Zelston and crossed the water-meadows – almost a sheet of water – to the Bere-Wimborne road and the long hill to Brimland Wood, above West Morden, and Bloxworth.

The hounds followed a burning scent. Leaving Bloxworth House and the village green to the west, she raced away towards the earths at Woolsbarrow and Pickard's Lookout. Then, swinging to the east, she entered the lowest end of Morden Park, beside Mr Drax's Decoy, and went straight through the plantation. The hounds then ran from scent to view and bowled her over in gallant style.

The distance was five miles, in 73 minutes, after breaking cover. The field fell behind after Bloxworth in heathland terrain that was largely unrideable.

PRESENTING THE PORTRAIT TO MR RADCLYFFE

One of the principal social highlights of Dorset's hunting calendar took place on 9 April 1874 when it was Charles Radclyffe's pleasant duty to receive a splendid portrait of himself and the pick of his pack of hounds. Those chosen to be so honoured were Lady-blush, Vengeance and Frantic in the front row, and behind them Dorcas, Laura, Watchful and Narrative. Mr Radclyffe's Hounds were painted by Stephen Pearce, as a commission funded by public subscription, which had raised £757-18s-0d from 215 donors.

The picture cost £530; engraving costs £185; the steel plate £20; and incidental expenses were £4-9s-0d. The residue of £18-9s-0d was given to the Hunt Servants' Benefit Society.

An early portrait study of Charles James Radclyffe of Hyde House, near Bere Regis,
dating from 1860. Peculiarities of dress include a whip apparently long enough
to be used as a walking stick.

Chapter Ten

SOUTH DORSET HOUNDS

LORD POLTIMORE ESTABLISHES THE SOUTH DORSET HUNT

 Lord Poltimore held his first meet with Cattistock-based South Dorset Fox Hounds at Sydling St Nicholas on 9 January 1859. Augustus Frederick George Warwick Bampfylde (1837–1908) succeeded his father, becoming the second Baron Poltimore in 1858. The same year he married Florence Sheridan, the daughter of Richard Brinsley Sheridan M.P. of Frampton Court. He owned a total of 20,000 acres, including Poltimore Park near Exeter, and would run his own pack of hounds until 1872, when he started to play his part in national life as Treasurer of the Household, followed by an active role in Conservative politics as Chancellor of the Primrose League.

BOATING END TO THE DASH FOR THE CHESIL BEACH

With Lord Poltimore and John Evans, the huntsman, the South Dorset Fox Hounds met at Buckland Wood, Buckland Ripers on 18 January 1863. They soon found and went away to West Chickerell, and then headed for the Fleet coast, via the big plantations, to Fleet House and Langton Herring. Here the cunning old customer led them over a nasty brook and through Wyke Wood and through the covers of Rodden and Elworthy.

They followed the Back Sea – as The Fleet lagoon is also known – all the way to Lord Ilchester's Decoy (Abbotsbury Swannery) where this remarkable fox decided, after seven miles, to swim for the Chesil Beach. Unluckily for him, there was a nearby boat with fishermen aboard, who followed him with one of the whips. He was brought back ashore for the last rites. Some clever foxes from Puncknowle and Bexington have been known to run the edge of a surf for a mile or more, leaving no scent for the hounds, before turning for the hills and home.

EIGHT MILES, FROM NETHER CERNE TO DRUCE

Meeting at Nether Cerne on 4 February 1863, the South Dorset Fox Hounds found in a hillside brake and broke away southwards for Forston Farm and the new Asylum (Herrison

Hospital, then officially known as the County Lunatic Asylum), a mile away from the old one. He went on to Charminster Clump and turned to cross the Old Sherborne Road to Lord Ilchester's brake and over the upper side of Burton Farm to Wolfeton Clump.

Facing the open, he went across Cocker's Frome Farm, and ran along Waterston Ridge and down Slyer's Lane, as if for Grey's Wood and Yellowham, but then went north to Lower and Higher Waterston. He crossed the meadows to the hedgerows of Druce Farm and continued over Muston Eweleaze and meadows. In sight of the hounds, he went to earth in a big rabbit warren on the downs, in Home Eweleaze. It had been a run of eight miles.

ESCAPE INTO WILD COUNTRY BETWEEN POWERSTOCK COMMON AND HOOKE PARK

The South Dorset Fox Hounds met at Higher Coombe, Litton Cheney, on 7 November 1864. They found in Coombe Coppice and went away up north-eastwards up Litton Hill, over Chalk Pit Lane and then the Bridport-Dorchester turnpike, towards Baglake Barn (demolished). Then he sunk into the deep valley to the west and went up Stancombe, northwards to ascend Eggardon Hill, and carried on straight ahead into the wild country beyond Powerstock Common.

They followed him through a series of hillside woods above Wytherstone, South Poorton, Burcombe and Coltleigh. The assumption was that he must have entered Hooke Park but the wind and rain was coming on and the scent became poor. The hounds just carried the line, around the hill, into Kingcombe Coppice where the run had to be abandoned after six miles. This was a good fox.

STEADY SIX MILES, FROM WYNFORD EAGLE TO THE HARDY MONUMENT

Meeting at Wynford Eagle on 4 March 1865, the South Dorset Fox Hounds found in the big coppice there, and went away over the eweleazes to the Winholes Coppice earths. These being blocked, he went over the hill to Compton Barn, and turned south over the Roman Road, to Kingston Russell Farm and the Dorchester-Bridport turnpike, leaving Long Bredy Hut to the west.

He continued straight ahead over the open downs, over the steep hill, on into Lower Kingston Russell. Here he turned eastwards and tried the large earths in Foxholes Coppice on the side of Sands Hill. These were also stopped. So he turned to the north-east, through Pitcombe on the west side of Bridehead House, and bore on over the hill to Winterbourne Plantation. Here he turned to the south-east and crossed the Steepleton Eweleaze towards the Hardy Monument.

He was pulled down in the open after a steady six miles. Lord Poltimore was much pleased. Jem Treadwell was out, as a guest staying at Cattistock, and helped huntsman John Evans with local knowledge. Reynard had done his best to save his brush.

STOPPED EARTHS AND THE CHESIL BEACH THWART A STOUT FOX

The 1846-built landmark of the Hardy Monument made for a conspicuous meet of the South Dorset Fox Hounds on 27 March 1865. They found in a pit on Black Down and made off northwards over Steepleton Cowleaze. Then they turned south-westwards, to Bridehead Farm, along Red Lane, and across Gorwell Farm, and in a big loop of wild country around Wears Hill, above Abbotsbury, to Ashley Chase.

He tried the big earths on Sands Hill, which were blocked, and went on again into the higher side of Puncknowle Wood. Here he was baffled again to find the main earths also stopped. So he turned again, across the coast road, and then followed it westwards on the seaward side. On reaching Limekiln Hill, below Puncknowle Lookout on the Knoll, he went down the slope into West Bexington and took to the Chesil Beach. This was also to no avail. He left the pebbles at East Bexington Farm, and crossed the fields behind the Preventive Station (The Old Coastguards) and was pulled down a mile away, almost having reached the holm oaks beside Abbotsbury Castle (the Ilchester family's seaside mansion, burned down in February 1913).

This classic run of nine miles, by a stout fox which had tried every dodge, was talked about for a long time afterwards.

DASHING YOUNG EARL TAKES OVER CATTISTOCK COUNTRY

Dudley Francis North, seventh Earl Guilford (1851–85), acceded to the mastership of the Cattistock Hounds on the retirement of Mr Codrington in 1882. The young and dashing son of Dudley, Lord North, from Weavering, Kent, succeeded to the earldom on the death of his grandfather in 1861, and entered the Royal Horse Guards. He married Georgina, second daughter of Sir George Chetwynd, in 1874, and had his family seat at Waldershare Castle, near Dover. In Dorset, having retired from the Army, he devoted himself to enjoying sport and facing the problems with the rural economy, becoming president of the Dorchester Agricultural Society.

An excellent horseman, he always led from the front, and had a popularity that started great and increased daily. Independently minded and nonsense-free, he was popular with ordinary people, as well as his peers.

LORD GUILFORD FATALLY INJURED IN DUNTISH FALL

Zoologist and botanist Charles William Dale invited the Cattistock Hounds into the heart of the Blackmore Vale, to meet at the Manor House, Glanvilles Wootton, on 19 December 1885, which turned out to be a fateful Friday. A fox was soon found in Seven Acres and was being followed at speed by a field led by their noble master, Lord Guilford, who appeared as plucky and energetic as ever. The difference was that his mount had not been ridden for four weeks.

It was fresh and restive. Refusing a fence, it threw its rider, who was unhurt and quickly back in the saddle again. The run continued in daring style, south-eastwards for two miles to Duntish, where they approached a six-feet high bank with a hedge on top and ditches either side.

The hedge had been recently plashed with double binders at the sides and earth in the middle. This made for a drop of eight feet. His lordship set the horse at this 'rasper' and its fore feet struck the soft top of the re-laid hedge, catching the hooves and causing it to somersault, with the horse on top with its feet in the air – though uninjured – and Lord Guilford thrown clear.

'I could not keep his head down,' his lordship said. Though conscious he was obviously seriously injured. He was placed on an iron gate and carried to the Castle Hill home of Thomas Holford, which was the nearest house, where he was examined by Dr William McEnery from Sherborne. He re-set broken limbs but was concerned that there were also serious internal injuries, including a ruptured intestine. 'I suppose I am in for six weeks at least,' his lordship remarked, as he ordered the hounds to be sent to Corscombe for the following day's meet.

The optimism was misplaced as delirium soon set in. Dr Kerr, from Cerne Abbas, had joined his colleague, and they now diagnosed a ruptured liver. An eminent surgeon, Professor Erichson, had been summoned from London. His lordship was moved home to Sydling Court, Sydling St Nicholas, but died shortly after nine o'clock that evening.

The coroner, Giles Symonds, decided that an inquest was unnecessary. He released the body for what became a remarkable display of public mourning. Nearly 120 sportsmen and friends, with 30 members of his lordship's household, accompanied the body in a solemn procession over the hills to the railway station at Maiden Newton. Colonel E.H.T. Digby and Captain E.W. Williams rode at the head of the cavalcade of huntsmen including

Nathaniel Surtees, from Child Okeford House, whose cousin was the creator of the immortal Jorrocks.

An even larger gathering awaited at Maiden Newton Station. They included Joseph Pearkes Fox Gundry, the Deputy Provincial Grand Master, and the rector of Maiden Newton, Rev. Montagu Hankey. The coffin was removed from the hearse and placed on a trestle. All the horsemen rode past it in succession to make their last farewell. It was then conveyed in silence to the train and Mr Gundry accompanied it on the journey to the family seat at Waldershare, Kent, where the deceased was interred. It was discovered later that the horse he was riding had defective sight with a cataract in each eye.

SNOWY SIX MILES, FROM DOLE'S HILL TO MILTON ABBAS

The Cattistock Hounds met at Druce, after a wild morning of snow and hail, at noon on 20 January 1890. The Master, Harry Rupert Fetherstonhaugh-Frampton of Moreton, missed the day due to illness, so command was assumed by Burtenshaw, the first whip. He found their first fox in the west-end hedgerows but this was soon lost. They then went north to Dole's Hill and the hogleazes. William Fookes found a fox in a pit close by.

This went away in the direction of Kingcombe and then south-east across the Cheselbourne farms and nearly to Chebbard Farm, where he crossed the Dorchester road and went over the down beside Dewlish Clump. He continued over the meadows and the Devil's Brook above Dewlish Mill and went over Wood's Down, south of West Bagber Copse, passing between Hewish Farm and Bagber Farm as he headed north-north-east to Luccombe and Windmill Clump.

Then he entered an area of turnips, jumped up in view, and went into the plantation at the top end of Milton Abbas village, where he was pulled down. It had been a good run of six miles in 80 minutes.

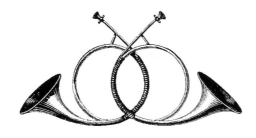

Edwardian elegance at a meet of the South Dorset Hunt at Broadwey,
near Weymouth, in the decade before the Great War.

Hounds, hunt staff and mounted and foot followers at an opening meet
of the South Dorset Hunt at Stinsford House in the late 1930s.

South Dorset hounds skirt the edge of Yellowham Wood, between Dorchester and
Puddletown, accompanied by a solitary terrier, circa 1938. They are across the
main road from Thomas Hardy's cottage birthplace.

The South Dorset Hounds meeting at Whitcombe, in a view looking
across the field to the church where William Barnes was parson.

The South Dorset Hounds meeting at Whitcombe in about 1930, having arrived in the Morris van.

The South Dorset Hounds meeting at Whitcombe and moving off along the main road, towards Broadmayne, with FX 5121 being the Dorset number plate on the first of the parked cars.

The South Dorset Hounds meeting on the village green at Tincleton, circa 1930. The land facing the parish church was then unfenced and unploughed.

Unusual prospect, though pictured for the horse rather than the rider, of a mounted
terrierman with the Cattistock or South Dorset hounds. Circa 1930.

THE CATTISTOCK HUNT

Left: Bronze-Age round barrows punctuate the skyline as the Cattistock huntsmen lead hounds past foot followers at Ridgeway Hill Gate, above Weymouth, circa 1938.

Above: Cattistock hounds move off past a newer form of transport at Coryates, Portesham, in about 1935.

Right: Looking akin to cavalry in the mud of the Somme, a dejected but resolute Cattistock field with collars turned up against the rain (which has also lashed Mr Seward's camera lens) at Langton Herring in the 1930s.

A mix of hunt staff, hounds and mounted and foot followers – plus at least one chauffeur – at a 1930s meet of the Cattistock at the now defunct crossroads of Stagg's Folly on the A37 above Sydling St Nicholas.

Onlookers, chauffeurs and hunt staff at a 1930s meet of the Cattistock at Toller Fratrum.

Cattistock hounds move away from a meet at Toller Porcorum in about 1930.

Meet of the Cattistock in woods above Bradford Peverell House in the 1930s.

With the outskirts of Weymouth in the background, beyond the haystacks,
Cattistock hounds move away from a meet at Upwey in the 1930s.

The Cattistock field move away on a sunny autumn morning, from Upwey Wishing Well, in 1925.

An indifferent Cattistock field watch idly as hounds draw a sizeable gorse,
on the downs above Upwey, circa 1935.

A large crowd of spectators at a meet of the Cattistock,
bringing the centre of Abbotsbury to a halt, in the 1930s.

The Cattistock field move away from a meet in 'Great Toller', now
generally known by its ancient name of 'Toller Porcorum'.

Left: Social interlude before the off for the Master, subscribers and foot followers of the Cattistock at Bradford Peverell in about 1930.

Above: Small girls on ponies are usually a feature of the hunting field, as at this 1930s meet of the Cattistock, at Up Cerne Wood.

Right: The lonely part of hunting – the Cattistock huntsman draws Portesham Rushes, in the 1930s.

With a number of motorised 'foot followers' in attendance,
Cattistock hounds move off from a meet on Portesham Hill, in 1935.

Reinforcing the bond between hounds and children,
the Cattistock at Portesham village, in 1935.

Another good study of Cattistock Hounds with the Master, huntsman and a
number of foot followers at Possum – the local name for Portesham – in 1935.

With hounds now in sight, the Cattistock field enjoy a canter along Bronkham Hill,
towards the Hardy Monument, in the 1930s.

A variety of transport, propelled both by equine and internal combustion means,
at a 1930s meet of the Cattistock at Frome St Quintin.

Right: You don't need a horse or pony – a donkey will suffice! 'We all hunt in Dorset,' was the contemporary caption, for this picture taken by Edwin Seward, at Coryates in 1935.

Above: Gentlemen subscribers and hunt staff enjoy a stirrup cup during a 1930s meet of the Cattistock Hunt at the now largely demolished Frampton Court.

Left: Hounds and hunt staff at a meet of the Cattistock behind Manor Farm, Godmanstone, in the 1930s.

The Cattistock move off from a meet in an unusual urban and military setting – being the barrack square of the depot of the Dorsetshire Regiment, Dorchester, in the 1930s.

A meet of the Cattistock at Wraxall Ridge, on the A356 between Maiden Newton and Winyard's Gap, circa 1938.

A carefully posed shot of the Cattistock Hounds and hunt staff at Chilfrome in the 1920s. Seven may seem an excessive number of employees. By the end of the century the hunt would have two.

A meet of the Cattistock at Upwey in the 1920s. Hounds, belying their supposed reputation for ferocity, adore human contact, especially that of children.

The Cattistock meeting at Cornhill, Dorchester, in the years before the Great War. Note the photographer with a plate camera (far left) risking life and limb on a ledge above the shop-front.

Left: Unimaginable today, bearing in mind current social mores and traffic conditions, the Cattistock draw hundreds to Cornhill, in the centre of Dorchester, in 1910.

Above: Behind a traditional iron and wood Dorset gate and with expertly thatched ricks in the background, the Cattistock huntsman holds up his hounds for Mr Seward's camera at a meet at Rodden, near Abbotsbury, in the 1930s.

Right: The Cattistock Hunt moves off across a pasture at Wrackleford, near Charminster, in the 1930s.

Left: Hunt staff and hounds pass thatched barns as they set off along the A37 at Wrackleford, between Stratton and Charminster, in the 1930s.

Right: Cattistock hunt staff and hounds at a post-war meet at Sydling St Nicholas. Roadside pipes may herald the arrival in the village of mains water.

Left: The Cattistock field pass the former Giants Head Inn above Cerne Abbas, c1930. The Inn now barely recognisable, was closed under the *Defence of the Realm Act* during the Great War, after persistent after-hours drinking was permitted by the landlord.

The Jacobean frontage of Wraxall Manor provides a backdrop to an opening
meet of the Cattistock Hunt, circa 1948.

The Cattistock Hunt meeting at the road junction in Evershot village, before the Great War
with Edwardian ladies (left) and Victorian matriarchs on the opposite side of the street.

The Cattistock field moves away into the hills above Evershot, in one of
Edwin Seward's earliest photographs, dating to before the Great War.

The Cattistock field moving through Sydling St Nicholas,
southwards down the valley, in the 1920s.

Hounds crossing the field (left) and the horses advancing along the lane,
as the Cattistock Hunt moves through Swyre.

The Cattistock Hounds setting off from Poxwell, along the A353.

Hounds in the grounds, beside Poxwell House, which provided a stylish
venue for this meet of the Cattistock Hunt.

The Cattistock Hounds meeting beside and below the arches of Grimstone Viaduct, near Stratton.

The Cattistock moving off from Grimstone, eastwards up Hog Hill,
with the Sydling Water and Lower Magiston in the background (right).

Thatched barn and traditional gate, with only the telegraph
pole to date this picture to Stratton in the 1920s.
The Cattistock to complete the timeless scene.

The Cattistock moving southwards through Stratton village,
towards Dorchester, along what was then the A37.

The Cattistock Hounds advancing along the A37, at Wrackleford, in the Frome Valley.

Bystanders watch from cottage doorways as the Cattistock huntsman brings his hounds
to the opening meet in the next parish, Maiden Newton, circa 1930.

Rare shot of a 1920s motor horsebox, one of the very first, attending this
Cattistock meet at Well Bottom, Piddletrenthide.

The Cattistock Hounds meeting at Well Bottom, Piddletrenthide,
around a sign which appears to dispute a right of way.

Holding back the pack. Cattistock hunt staff keep control,
on a gorse-covered downland hilltop, while the terrierman is summoned.

A young follower watches as the Cattistock Hounds are held on Portesham Hill in 1930.

Gone to ground. The terrierman sets to work as dismounted members of the Cattistock field look on.

'A kill with the Cattistock,' the contemporary caption reads, circa 1935.

Friendly beagles, meeting village boys in Cattistock, in a scene from the 1920s.

The Fox and Hounds Inn at Cattistock witnessing a case of
hare and hounds as the Eton College Beagles move off.

Hare hunting, with a kill for the visiting Eton College Beagles, in the heart of Cattistock country.

Chapter Eleven

BLACKMORE VALE COUNTRY

IRREGULAR PACKS BECOME THE BLACKMORE VALE HOUNDS

 The tradition of Blackmore Vale hunting grew out of a succession of irregular personal packs. The almost impossible extent of Mr Farquharson's country from 1806 to 1858 allowed other gentlemen to start their own hunts. These included Rev. Harry Farr Yeatman at Stock Gaylard, Lydlinch, from 1826, and Henry Hall at Holbrook House, near Wincanton, from 1831. The latter, who was described as 'a fine horseman and a fearless and straight rider', relinquished a portion of his country, towards Bryanston, to Mr Portman during the 1830s.

Mr Drax bought Mr Portman's Hounds in 1840 and effectively became Master of the whole of Blackmore Vale country as well as his own Charborough Hounds territory in south-east Dorset. In 1853, Mr Drax sold his pack to George Whieldon of Wyke Hall, Gillingham. He shared the mastership of the Blackmore Vale Hounds with Captain Stanley and Viscount Dungarvan from 1853 to 1855. Lord Harry Thynne of Longleat was the Master in 1855–56, followed by Mr R. Strachey for 1856–57, and Captain Stanley for 1857–58.

Then George Wingfield Digby, the squire of Sherborne Castle, took the reins from 1858 to 1865, usually in the first flight and never happier than when on his fine chestnut Magic. He delighted in a gallop and never tired of jumping. Mr Digby perfected fast riding over the Vale and would be accompanied home by his faithful henchman, Dick Anderson, in the days when Sherborne was such a squalid town that a clergyman remarked that having lived there over twelve years he had never seen a frog and just one toad, on account of 'the vast quantity of rats with which the town is infested.'

Mr Wingfield Digby liked big hounds – with the pace and stamina for a good gallop – and introduced the Belvoir Guider blood into the Blackmore Vale kennels (1851). By 1860 there were six and half couple of Guider's offspring in the pack. Of these, three and half couple were bred by Lord Portsmouth and came to Mr Digby in a draft. Guider was by Mr Drake's

Duster, and through his dam Gamesome (1845) strained back through Rasselas (1831) and Saladin (1813), both of which hounds were much used at Belvoir, to Dancer, which sired every hound entered in the old Belvoir kennel book for 1796. Another line in Mr Digby's kennels in 1858 could be traced through seven-year-old Solomon, a son of Saucebox (1846), grandson of Lord Portman's Spitfire, which was much used as a sire by Mr Drax in the closing years of his mastership.

John Press (1818–85), a former whipper-in with Mr Farquharson's Hounds, was brought back from the Cambridgeshire by Mr Digby to be his huntsman, in 1863. The Prince of Wales (later King Edward VII) had been out with them when he was at Cambridge University. He presented Press with a £5 note and a photograph in gratitude for a great run; both were framed and hung over the Press family's sitting-room mantelpiece. Press himself had arrived as damaged goods, on crutches from a riding accident, and began his first season in Dorset and Somerset wearing one boot and a slipper. His control of the hounds, with a deep gruff voice, was absolute. He preferred dark-coloured hounds, saying they had a hardier constitution, with the further advantage in the muddy country of the Blackmore Vale that they could be well splattered without it showing.

Failing health caused Mr Wingfield Digby to make over his whole establishment of horses, hounds and servants, together with the kennels at Charlton Horethorne, to Sir Richard Glyn (1824–1905). A veteran of Empire conflicts, from the Kaffir War through to Lucknow, he lived at Gaunt's House, Hinton Martell, near Wimborne. He became Master of the Blackmore Vale Hounds from 1865 to 1884 with John Press continuing as huntsman until 1876 when George Orbell took over.

Mr Digby had introduced Ruby in a draft of hounds, apparently from Sir Watkin Wynn, in 1864. She proved to be the foundation of the late-nineteenth century pack, beginning with her mating in Sir Richard Glyn's mastership with Lord Poltimore's Voyager (1867), the son of the Duke of Beaufort's Voyager. No less than four couple were entered in the kennel register for 1868. Another lasting influence was from two couple by Lord Portsmouth's Commodore with Mr Villebois' Matchless (1863) to which many of the best hounds of latter times date back. Matchless had come to Sir Richard in 1865 and was by Marmion with Willing. She would be second only to Ruby in her influence on the pack.

A particular favourite with huntsman John Press was dog-hound Lasher (1866), which came in a draft from Lord Portman, and had an immense bone structure. 'Like that of a horse,' Press used to boast. He was one of a capital litter by Lord Poltimore's Lifter with Lord Portman's Rapid and was ousted from his home kennel because of his disproportionate size.

After the departure of John Press in 1876, one of the hounds, Russian, remained loyal to the old huntsman and kept looking for him. One day he attached himself to Sir Julius Glyn who happened to be on a horse that used to be ridden by Press.

John Press went slowly at his fences and used to say 'you can squeeze through anywhere'. Another of his favourite sayings, to anyone bemoaning the absence of a kill, was 'Yes,' followed by a pause. 'Yes, the glorious uncertainty of fox-hunting.' He had married for a second time and lived with his wife and young children, appropriately including Nimrod and Diana for the god and goddess of the hunt, at the former Bugle Inn, on the opposite side of the railway line from Milborne Port Station. He suffered epileptic fits and was diagnosed insane, being removed to the County Asylum, where he died on 27 December 1885. One of the memorial cards read: 'Alas, he's gone to Earth at last; Waiting for the Trumpet's blast!'

At the suggestion of John Wingfield Digby – the largest landowner and fox-preserver in Blackmore Vale country – when Sir Richard Glyn retired in 1884 he was succeeded by Thomas Merthyr Guest (1838–1904) of Inwood, Henstridge. He had moved there from Fifehead Magdalen after marrying hunting horsewoman Lady Theodora Grosvenor, daughter of the second Marquess of Westminster, in 1877. She was then living at Motcombe House with her mother, Elizabeth the Marchioness of Westminster, who was also renowned for her prowess in the field. Lady Theodora once broke her leg against a gate which swung closed, causing her to lament her luck in having to collide with the only gatepost in all Dorset that was not rotten. She insisted on continuing to ride but went home via Dr Long's at Stalbridge and told him to follow her to Inwood with some splints. Lady Theodora was the founder and principal benefactor of the Hunt Servants' Benefit Society which began its work in 1872.

When Churchill Langdon, the Master of the Seavington Harriers, made an after-lunch speech at a Blackmore Vale puppy-show he complimented Lady Theodora on her extensive knowledge of hounds, which was all the more remarkable because in his experience 'ladies find it very difficult to distinguish one hound from another.' He knew this to be the case as in his pack there used to be just one black-and-tan: 'Ladies who were anxious to show their interest in the hounds, were always constant in their inquiries after this one. He is no more and questions are now of a most general nature. No other hound is ever asked after by name.'

Mr Guest retained the mastership of the Blackmore Vale Hounds for the remainder of the century and though of heavy-weight frame always led from the front, saying it was safer to be the first at a fence than second, believing 'that a horse is more likely to use his eyes well when he has only himself to rely on than when he is following another.' The Master and servants wore scarlet and were always mounted on grey horses.

The hounds, a mixed pack, were devotedly attached to Mr Guest, to the extent that they would sometimes break away from the whipper-in and scramble all over the Master's carriage. Generally they were light in colour, with tan markings, as Mr Guest thought they looked the best when running. They were bred for nose and voice and were said to have the deepest note of any pack in land. He never had less than a hundred couple in kennels and would sometimes declare himself to be the owner of one of the biggest packs in the world. He would hunt six days a week for a period of nearly 30 years.

They were distinctive in having unrounded ears, as Mr Guest bucked the fashion, and none was mute. Lexicon, a fine hound that came in a draft, ran mute from Holwell Gorse in 1886 and was never taken out again. In the field he banned the practice of 'holloaing' – ordering his men never to do it – on the grounds that 'you can always get hounds' heads up, but you cannot depend on getting them down again on the spot you want.'

The honorary secretary to the Blackmore Vale Hunt from 1863, in the time of George Wingfield Digby's mastership, until retirement through ill health in 1896, was Rev. Samuel Dendy of Lattiford House, Holton.

ELEVEN-MILE RUN FROM PLUMBER ENDS WITH ESCAPE IN DEWLISH PARK STABLES

The Blackmore Vale Hounds met at the Green Man, King's Stag, on 27 March 1864 and drew two miles to the south, across the River Lydden, in Humber Wood. The huntsman, Jack Press, was riding a little iron grey, 15 hands high, which had been bought by Mr Wingfield Digby for £15, from between the shafts of a butcher's cart in Malvern Wells, where he used to stay most summers. They found a good straight fox which took them across a few fields with double hedges into Short Wood and over the road from Castle Hill to Mappowder.

He then put his head over the stiff country southwards towards Alton Common and went up on to the chalklands through Armswell, to turn south-east beside the Fox Inn, Plush (where the hostelry is now the Brace of Pheasants) and cross the steep hill to Lyscombe. He then ran south across the downland to Dole's Ash and bore east from there over more open country to the lower end of Cheselbourne parish. Crossing the road, leaving Chebbard Farm to the south, he crossed to Tuck's Down and went over the Dewlish road, turning south to run the enclosures at the back of the parish, into Shale's Farm and Field Marshal Sir John Michel's 150-acre Dewlish Park.

Here he vanished, in the region of the large gardens and the stable-block, where Jack Press cast around for half an hour. They then gave up, after eleven miles, and made for home.

The sequel, the following morning, happened as the groom and his helpers opened the stable door. Out shot the fox – which had been lying under the manger.

NEW HUNTSMAN'S TWENTY-MILE TREK, FROM ROOKSMOOR TO GILLINGHAM

Turner, from Lord Portsmouth's pack, was the new huntsman of the Blackmore Vale Hounds who was out with them for the first time on 10 January 1866 when they met at the Green Man, King's Stag. They found in Rooksmoor and went off eastwards to Deadmoor Common, then straight as an arrow northwards for Bagber Common in three miles. Bearing a little to the left, the fences big and the enclosures small, the hounds were some way in front of the horses until they reached the River Stour at King's Mill.

Here there was a long check, which let a great part of the field catch up, and the hounds were on the line again, in a narrow lane. This took them into fields, to pass Marnhull and Manston, with Fontmell Parva to the south, as he then turned and headed north to the outskirts of Gillingham. Either the scent had changed or they were on to a fresh fox. Either way it was too late to go further so the hounds were stopped after 20 miles.

Henry Symonds accompanied Mr Hambro home – after an hour's rest at Sturminster Newton – in a dark ride across Sturminster Common and over Belchalwell Hill, to Milton Abbey. This was reached at eight o'clock and Symonds was provided with a liquor-up and a first-rate cigar, which he smoked on the final three miles to Milborne St Andrew, with a tired horse.

CLEVER CHECK CONCLUDES 'GLORIOUS GALLOP' FROM TEMPLECOMBE

The kennel meet of the Blackmore Vale Hounds, at Charlton Horethorne on 25 March 1875, found in North Side Wood, Templecombe. They settled down to run the flat pastures north-eastwards to Cucklington and Shanks House where the Grant-Daltons lived. Here they checked, after a straight four miles in 35 minutes. John Press cast around the house and persevered for some time. Then the hounds found the line and the hunted fox jumped up in view and gave another fast 15 minutes before he was rolled over in the open.

The huntsman, in his last season, was given the credit for the skill with which he re-found their elusive quarry. Among those taking part in this 'glorious gallop' were the Master, Sir Richard Glyn, Arthur Dendy, Captain John Luttrell, Captain Harry Farr Yeatman, Mr Pepys and Mr H. Poole.

WEATHER AND THE UP-TRAIN STOP SPORT AT BUCKHORN WESTON TUNNEL

The day following the Agricultural Show at Gillingham, the Blackmore Vale Hounds met at Stock Hill House, to be welcomed and warmed by Colonel and Mrs Philip Wride Matthews on a bitterly cold 25 November 1884. Mr and Mrs Plowden, the new residents at Wyke, joined on foot. Ringrove and Sandley covers drew blank but an old fox was found in nearby turnips. He made for Langham and back towards Stock Hill, going via Ringrove, to Tunnel Plantation, where a check occurred. A 'holloa' put them on the line again and he went to ground in the railway embankment. He was dug out and devoured in a snowstorm.

Then the up-train came round the corner out of Buckhorn Weston Tunnel and almost ran into the middle of the pack. The driver applied his powerful vacuum brake – no doubt much to the surprise of the passengers – and stopped the train with hounds crossing both before and behind the train. None was injured but hunting was abandoned due to the deteriorating weather.

FOXING AROUND MR DRAX'S SECOND HOME

The new Master of the Blackmore Vale Hounds, Thomas Merthyr Guest, and his wife Lady Theodora Guest, of Inwood, Henstridge, held a bye-day at Folke village on 26 November 1884. They drew Mr Drax's covers there, by his request, as the former owner of the Charborough Hounds was now living at Holnest Park. The Master and Lady Theodora attended with General Alfred Fox Place, from Thornford, and Mr Clayton.

Broke Wood contained more than one fox. Another went away from Butterwick Wood for Withy Tree Copse and Ferney Down. The hounds worked steadily on a cold line with almost beautifully slow hunting. They went by Buckshaw and Holwell House to the plantations where they ran out of scent as the day came to a close.

SINGLE-HANDED, WILDFIRE CATCHES HIS FOX AT MIDDLEMARSH

Another small field met the dog-pack of the Blackmore Vale Hounds at Holnest Pound on the soaking morning of 2 December 1884. They soon found two foxes in Longburton Gorse but lost them in indifferent scent. Another went from Little Stockbridge covers, beside the Stockbridge Oak, south-eastwards for Six Ash Common. Then it turned west to the Home Bushes and from there ran south for the length of it to Bailey Ridge. With a burning scent it turned south-east beside the milestone and passed the gorse at White House Farm, to go on through Higher Sweethills, White House Common, then into Admiral Digby's Plantation.

They galloped up its broad grass ride and went from there, without a pause, to Remedy, in 28 minutes. A timely check enabled the horses to gather their wind. George Orbell, the huntsman, soon had the hounds on line again.

They continued beyond Hermitage, into Grange Woods, where a single hound, Wildfire, had a paws-on encounter with their fox in an open drain. Having been thus dislodged, Wildfire chased him round a field at Middlemarsh, knocking him over once or twice, and then brought him to bay in the trench. George Orbell called a 'holloa' to bring the rest of the pack and then handed them this full-grown dog fox, after three miles and 59 minutes.

'A BAD DAY FOR HUNTING BUT WORSE FOR ANYTHING ELSE'

It was also a small field that gathered for the Blackmore Vale Hounds at Haydon Lodge in driving rain on 4 November 1884. It was intensely cold as they waited in the friendly shelter of Sherborne Park wall. Captain and Mrs Alexander Fownes Luttrell were out, having returned from East Quantoxhead during the week. It was a potentially disappointing day, with a gale and a falling barometer, but the hounds ran for four hours and thoroughly rattled Haydon Gorse, Tripps, Deadman's Copse, Goathill, Muse Hill and Hanover Wood, though without result.

They then repeated a widening circle, by running as far west as Snagharbour Wood at North Wootton, and back again to Sherborne Park where they had a fast run for a few minutes until a deer foiled the line. They then went along the top of the park to the Holts but had lost the scent.

A second fox took them eastwards to Goathill and Hanover Wood, where a fresh one crossed the line and was followed northwards for a couple of miles, through the walled garden of Ven House, to East Hill, above Milborne Port. The very weak line was then followed to the eastwards for another mile, to Toomer Hill, where they whipped off and went home to nearby Inwood. 'It's been a bad day for hunting, but a worse one for anything else,' Lady Theodora Guest remarked.

The day would be remembered for the meeting between the Master, Thomas Merthyr Guest, and an urchin with a frantic sheep-dog on the road between Goathill and Milborne Port, at Tinker's Cross. Had he seen their fox? 'Yah, sir, he be gone across the ground.' Which way? 'Across ground, sir.' Which way was his head? 'Straight in front of him, sir.' Ugh was the Master's response as the hounds hit off the line and the boy's assistance was no longer required.

SHORT RUNNING FOX GOES BACK TO START NEAR FONT LE ROI

A moderate field met the Blackmore Vale Hounds at Font le Roi, as the Caundle Marsh crossroads at Marsh Court is now known, on 8 December 1884. Lord Digby was out with his daughter, two sons and a grandson. Walter Long had come from Wiltshire.

The dog pack found in Ferney Down Wood and ran merrily south-westwards to Broke Wood, and through Withy Tree Copse. They went over the fields and fences, softened by recent rains, to head eastwards over the Caundle Brook and to ground in Buckshaw Brake. The couple of miles had taken 25 minutes.

They came to a halt and were discussing the Fabian Society and the Redistribution Bill as the fox bolted and swam the stream, after some hesitation, then went half way up Portdown Hill and into the shelter of Marsh Copse. The weak line went north by Font le Roi and up to the Holts, and was then lost after a second couple of miles, in the flat below Dead Man's Copse. They then went westwards to Snagharbour Wood and then for a mile southwards to the other side of Alweston where they ran a ring round by Ferney Down Copse, till he went to ground near his starting point.

The Master, Thomas Merthyr Guest, sent the field home but stayed to dig him out and kill him.

RIVER-CROSSING FOX WINS AFTER SEVEN MILES AROUND STURMINSTER

A bright sunny morning brought out a large field for the Blackmore Vale Hounds on 13 December 1884 when they met at Bagber Bridge, Sturminster Newton. Yeargrove, Spar Copse and two little covers at Hinton St Mary were drawn blank. They went on to Twinwood Coppice, where the busy little lady pack spoke to a fox, which broke out eastwards and crossed the Marnhull-Sturminster road to Spar Copse, then looping round for a mile to Spar Coppice on the north side of Hinton village. Here he was headed by a dog and turned short back.

He ran over the road, eastwards to Cut Mill, after a mile of stiff country. Some of the hounds crossed the River Stour to Pentridge Farm but the huntsman, George Orbell, re-called them by horn. They then ran southwards through the lower part of Twinwood, for the third mile, and out on the Hewstock side, to the gates of the Sturminster Union Workhouse.

He went on down to Chivrick's Brook, where the water jumpers had the best of it – ignoring the nearby bridge – and went on past Manston Copse and down to the River Stour, which was forded. Thanks were expressed to the Master, Mr Guest, for this was one of his many well-marked fords.

Then, after his fourth mile, he turned south-west towards the Bull Inn at Newton and made good his way into Piddles Wood and ran back along it, to re-cross his line at Rose's Mill at Fiddleford and escape back to his home side of the river and Manston where he went to ground in a trip under a gateway. By that time the pack had found another weak line towards Hinton, news came about the location of their hunted one, but they were too late as he had just emerged from the trip and slipped in front of them through the hedgerows to the river. Here he disappeared, yet again, after frustrating them for six or miles and 170 minutes.

KENNEL MEET GOES TO BAGBER COMMON

It was a frosty morning when the Blackmore Vale Hounds were greeted by a large field at their Kennels in Charlton Horethorne on 16 December 1884. Among them were the Hon. Miss Digby and Major Hon. Francis Baring (1850–1915). The pack failed to find in Milborne Slates, Poyntington Withybed, Southern Hill or Everlanes.

They headed east to Spurles and found a fox there which ran for Toomer Hill and looped round back to Spurles Covert for the first two miles. He was chased out again and ran around Red House Farm and Bowden hamlet and yet again to Toomer Hill, having now gone four miles.

This time he decided to try his fortune further afield. He went south-eastwards, into Dorset, and through Frith Wood and Pile Wood to Holtham Plantation. Here, south of Stalbridge, he was thought to have gone to ground, but the hounds had no hesitation in putting a strong head over the Stock plough-lands, beside South Common Plantation, and attempted entering Stock Wood. Another four miles, this time of real running, had been achieved.

Being headed, he turned eastwards, for Lydlinch, and crossed the River Lydden as if for Puxey. Instead, he swung back through the brick-kiln (Brickyard Farm) and went north-east across Bagber Common. Here the hounds were whipped off, conveniently beside the Wincanton-Blandford road, after a total run of ten miles in 153 minutes.

EXCITED HOUND BITES THE HUNTSMAN INSTEAD OF THE FOX

The Master, Thomas Merthyr Guest, had to take over control of the pack at the meet of the Blackmore Vale Hounds at Totnell Corner, Leigh, on 18 December 1884. It was a wet and wild day which started with a sharp 14 minutes from finding in Totnell Gorse, to Bide's Gorse, where George Orbell, the huntsman, put his hands on their first fox. As he was throwing it to the hounds, one of them missed the target and put his teeth through Orbell's hand. He had to go home.

Another was then found and lost in Whitfield Woods. A third was found in Tipples and ran well to Thornford Firs, by Conway's Gorse, to Whitfield and back again to Conway's Gorse, and then to Leweston Wood. Having gone up and down it, he then went into the Little Gorse, and under the wall into Lillington Wood, back to Leweston, and on to ground by the park wall. Leaving the master to dig him out, the field turned for home, and were caught in a thunderstorm.

GENERAL PARKE PROVIDES A HANDSOME BREAKFAST AND AN INSTANT FOX

General William and Mrs Anna Parke and their son made everyone welcome at the meet of the Blackmore Vale Hounds at Thornhill House, Stalbridge, on 20 December 1884. It was a handsome breakfast for a stormy day. The master did not move off until General Parke (1822–97, knighted 1887), a veteran of Crimea and the Indian Mutiny, and Aide-de-Camp to Queen Victoria, had mounted and all were ready for the work of the day.

This began in one of the nearby covers and the hounds swept down the hill, eastwards towards Bagber Common and across the River Lydden, leaving the field the options of a deep ford or a detour via Bagber Bridge. They kept in sight and then made a short ring around a hedgerow on Ralph's Farm and ran into him there after only 15 minutes. Mr Guest, the Master, had to break up the fox himself as Orbell was unable to make much use of his hound-damaged hand (see 18 December 1884 entry).

They then drew Holtham Plantation and found close by, in Sturt Coppice, and had a slow run back to Thornhill where they lost. Their third fox, from Stalbridge Common Plantation, was followed by instinct rather than scent, in a slow and patient hunt that marked him to ground near Stourton Caundle. He was dug and eaten.

A fourth fox trotted from the same earth but the hounds had to be stopped, with considerable difficulty, as it was now too dark to do any more.

NIGHT SAVES A HONEYCOMBE BRUSH, ON DUNTISH COMMON

Boxing Day 1884 saw the Blackmore Vale Hounds meet with a goodly assemblage ranging from carriages and traps to boys on foot at Westhill Gate (now West Hill Lodge), above Sherborne. They spent the morning riding up and down in Honeycombe Wood after a brace of foxes which provided entertainment rather than their brushes.

The master then trotted through Green Lane cover and a fox broke away for Westhill, over the little brook, and then raced south for Leweston Park, the Rookery and Leweston Wood. He then turned for Whitfield Woods and went into the Holm Bushes. After a momentary check a hound picked out the line in the field, across the Leigh road, from where Orbell's ringing cheer brought the rest of the pack up. With noses down, and an occasional word from the leading hound, they carried on to Gaulpits and the back of Holnest Park, through Holnest churchyard, and on south-eastwards to Berkeley Gorse.

Here they turned north-east, still running well, over Butterwick Brook, and on to Boys Hill. Approaching here, a stiff piece of timber provided an opportunity for youthful ardour to show itself off. One gentleman, on getting over, found himself sitting on his saddle on the ground as his horse picked itself up. Dirty coats betrayed others, showing that they had not been in vertical motion all of the day, and nor was it over.

From Boys Hill they went north-eastwards, close to Buckshaw House and Holwell, and then turned south for Round Chimneys Farm. From here they went on more slowly almost to the Glanvilles Wootton covers. These he had not touched, but made his way, still slowing, over Newland Farm and Duntish Common, where within hope of success daylight failed and the hounds were stopped. They had covered nine miles in 100 minutes.

From Sherborne Park to Holwell (and back)

The New Year's Day meet of the Blackmore Vale Hounds in 1885 came as an inevitable anti-climax, after an old-fashioned run across Somerset of 248 minutes, but that is another story. It took them from Jack White's Gibbet, near Wincanton, to between North Wootton and Barrow, towards Wells, where the fox jumped into the apron of an old woman who was guarding the door of her cottage, and the hounds killed him at her feet as he fell back out of the apron.

The first meet of the year, back in Dorset, was at Haydon Lodge. Nevertheless it was off to a good start, with two foxes accounted for in Sherborne Park.

Eventually, their third fox decided to go a little further, being off southwards to Snagharbour and Folke church, though hardly at any pace. He then went on past Butterwick Wood, to Boys Hill and Gog and Magog, the giant oak trees near Somerset Gate Cottage; a reminder that Holwell was a detached parish of that county until its transfer to Dorset (in 1844).

There he turned back by Holwell Plantations and quickened his pace, up wind, as the hounds pressed him, to Ferney Down Wood and Alweston, back towards Sherborne Park and home. Daylight was going and nothing more could be done with him. He had tantalised them across eight miles and had their attention for 130 minutes.

TOO MANY FOXES SPOIL THE BROTH, AT FIVE BRIDGES

The meet of the Blackmore Vale Hounds at Five Bridges, at Nyland, below Kington Magna, was attended by Mr Digby Collins on one of his flying visits. Other borderland friends were also present to see the first fox found and killed in a cover at Fifehead Magdalen. The next, from the lower cover, took them up through the Avenue, and eastwards round by the front of the house, to Stour Provost and Hayes Copse where he went to ground, after 24 minutes.

The third fox came from Fifehead Withybed and went briskly up to the wood and over Hiscock's Farm, then back and under the wood, across to Highbridge Mill – this time fording the River Stour – and was lost in Ashley Plantation. The weather was cold and the scent indifferent.

Then they trotted a mile or so to Prior's Down, to find their fourth fox, which headed off for Stalbridge and turned northwards beside the town. Having followed the Somerset and Dorset Railway to Henstridge Station he then turned eastwards for Bow Brook and crossed the Sherborne-Shaftesbury road, for Nyland and Five Bridges. Here, back at what had been the starting point for the day, it was obvious that there was more than one fox in front. Too many cooks spoil the broth, but the last gallop had been an invigorating 45 minutes.

TWO MIDDLEMARSH RUNS STOPPED BY FROSTY HILLSIDES

Meeting at the White Horse, Middlemarsh, and moving into Grange Woods opposite, the Blackmore Vale Hounds threw themselves busily into the cover, on 17 January 1885. They were soon streaming off, northwards, to Butterwick Brook, and then east to Glanvilles Wootton. Here their fox must have been headed, back to Round Chimneys Farm, and then up the brook again to Little Butterwick. Six of the field had the best of it, with three jumping it, and the other three fording.

The pace was slow and the rest soon caught up, before reaching Holnest Park, and heading on south-westwards to Sweethills and Castle Plantation at Three Gates, where they ran out of scent after two hours.

From here they trotted on to Bide's Gorse, where they found, and ran sharply through the Hilfield covers and towards the chalk escarpment. They were whipped off the foot of it, for the master well knew it would be slippery, still being frost-bound on these north-facing slopes.

Those remaining in the field returned to Grange Woods and spent 90 minutes in a circuit of Grange, Gore and Prince's Wood. They then went off across open country to Remedy and Up Cerne Wood but had to be stopped again before reaching frosty hills.

IN AND AROUND HOLWAY AND TRENT

Meeting at White Post Gate, Higher Oborne, on 19 January 1885, the lady pack of the Blackmore Vale Hounds drew hedges and turnip fields at Gifford's Coombe Farm. They reached Harthill and Holway before the first fox was found. It went off to the south-west, up Charlock Hill, and was lost in the rough, hilly country.

They then drew Trent Barrow and found close by, in Trent Gully, from which two fine foxes departed. One was followed to the Great Western Railway branch line from Yeovil to Castle Cary. Here there was a check, which showed that the hounds had not crossed the line, and that their fox had doubled back to the gully. He was persuaded to run again, this time crossing the line westwards, to Adber hamlet, where he turned north for Rimpton. The brook beside the mill required some negotiation, due to its awkward banks, and the field was rewarded with a view of the hounds streaming south-eastwards, into arable lands at Sandford Orcas where they lost what little scent they had been following.

Recovering the line, his tracks were followed up Harthill again, and on almost to Clatcombe Barn. A run of 120 minutes had brought them to very near where they had begun.

FIFTH FOX RUNS FALLING HORSES TO STANDSTILL AT BUCKHORN WESTON

Those who got up early enough, after the Sherborne Ball, joined the Blackmore Vale Hounds at their Henstridge Ash meet on 22 January 1885. The time was half an hour later than usual and a large party had rubbed their eyes and gathered together. Visitors included the ex-Master, Sir Richard Glyn from Gaunt's House, Hinton Martell, and the present Master, Thomas Merthyr Guest, who carried the horn in the absence of George Orbell, who was hors de combat from a heavy fall.

They drew Lady Theodore's Gorse on their home territory of Inwood. He went away on the far side but turned for the Somerset and Dorset Railway and was headed into the hounds' mouths. Nyland, to the east, was the next draw, and their second fox ran away northwards, over the River Cale, and was followed via a useful ford, towards Buckhorn Weston. He then turned south-eastwards, to Kington Magna, where the hounds threw up their heads at the Rectory gate and he was found to have gone to ground in a drain, after 35 minutes.

Going on to Rodgrove they came upon a sleeping fox, almost too quickly, as his first whimper proved to be his death-knell. Their fourth fox, moments after they had eaten the last, proved much livelier. He broke cover for Marsh Farm and went past Perrett's Farm, to Grove Withybed and across the River Cale, which had to be jumped in and out of – for want of a ford – with the result that the first whip, Tom Jordan, got wet through.

He went on through Horwood Farm and Stileway but turned there for some reason, via Writh, to return to Stileway. He then went over Coneygore Hill, pointing for Bayford, but turned south down Cucklington Bottom.

As the pace was beginning to show on the horses, this gallant fox gathered speed, around Shanks House to Clinger Farm. Here Mr Dalton Foster Grant-Dalton, from Shanks, spared the horses by opening some invaluable gates. The line was followed beside Weston Wood and into Quarr Hollow, Buckhorn Weston, where not only was it lost, but the horses were so pumped after this demanding run of eight difficult miles in 100 minutes that none of them could have followed. Tom Jordan's was far from being the only fall; none was serious, and everyone from Dorsetshire regarded it as a rare treat to be riding on top of the ground in January.

The roll-call of Blackmore Vale followers included Nathaniel Surtees of Child Okeford House, whose cousin was the creator of Jorrocks, with his daughter who married another stalwart, Charles Phelips. Major Dugdale was generally out during visits to his uncle at Sherborne Castle when he could come down from Staff College at Sandhurst. Others as listed by Miss Alys F. Serrell were Sir Julius Glyn; Lieutenant-Colonel John Goodden of Compton House, Over Compton; Colonel Edward Chadwick from Chetnole; Mr and Mrs Clayton from Bradford Abbas; Captain and Mrs Alexander Fownes Luttrell of Court House, East Quantoxhead; Captain Scobell; John Bradney of Bayford Lodge, Stoke Trister; Rev. William Marriott Leir and sons from Ditcheat; Major Harbin; William Ernest Brymer M.P. of Ilsington House, Puddletown, with his brother, Rev. John Brymer, from Child Okeford; Colonel Leopold Paget of Park Homer, Hampreston; Dr William McEnery of Semington House, Sherborne; Captain Grissell; Major Orred and his brother, Stanley Orred; Charles Chichester; Mr Robertson; Major and Mrs McAdam; Colonel Mount Batten; Cavendish Bentinck and his sons from Brownsea Island; Rev. Frederick Tyrwhitt-Drake from Pulham; Major-General Hamilton Forbes of Heale House, Curry Rivel; Worshipful Thomas Englesby Rogers of Yarlington House; Giles Hussey; Wills Sandford of Compton Castle; William Connop of the Manor House, Fifehead Neville; George Allen; Major-General William Waller of Grosvenor Lodge, Sherborne; and (Sir) Godfrey Lagden from Stock Rectory, when he was home from Africa where his colonial service covered conflicts from the Cape to Cairo with big-game shooting interludes.

'LOVELY LINE' ENDS WITH POOR SCENT IN LADY THEODORA'S GORSE

It was a very different day, after the rain, when the Blackmore Vale Hounds met at Bagber Bridge, Sturminster Newton, on 24 January 1885. They drew uneventfully in Bagber Copse, Queen's Coppice, Sir Richard's Gorse, and the adjoining spinneys. They went on up the Stour to King's Mill withybed, at Marnhull, and then turned north-west, to Prior's Down at Stalbridge.

Here they found at last, after more than one fox ran from shelter at the sound of the horn, and one led them a lovely line under Stalbridge and northwards by Bellman's Cross to Lady Theodora's Gorse between Whitchurch and Higher Nyland, where in poor scent the pace was slow. It took 30 minutes for him to shake off his pursuers. Another brace was found in Stalbridge Park but nothing could be done with them.

FOX LOST AS IT FALLS WITH HOUNDS INTO THE CAUNDLE BROOK

The Green Man, King's Stag, meet of the Blackmore Vale Hounds on 27 January 1885 led to the unfailing Rooksmoor cover. From here a good one left at a great pace, for Lydlinch Common, then north-west to Bagber Common and Bagber Bridge. Here he crossed the River Lydden and headed west, to Thornhill, but the scent was failing and they lost him towards Drakes.

Another was found in Lydlinch Withybed and gave a ten-minute gallop before going to ground. He was persuaded to leave and crossed the river to Stock House where he was pulled down beside the Caundle Brook, beyond the park. Hounds and fox fell backwards together, into the water, and the latter was lost in the wild confusion.

PLAYING 'ROUGE ET NOIR' IN THE BROOK AT WHITFIELD WOODS

The gale had subsided when the Blackmore Vale Hounds met at Westhill Gate (now West Hill Lodge) above Sherborne on 3 February 1885. There was, however, no scent and therefore not much prospect of a run. This was proved by the first fox, from Honeycombe Wood, which ran the length of the cover, sinking the hill at the western end, and turned up again towards Clifton Wood. He had to be lost – or saved, as he would look at it – near Beer Hackett.

Their second fox was found in Tibble's Copse and with the hounds close he made off eastwards across Knighton Lane to Whitfield Woods. The brook intervened and though narrow it afforded scope for a game of 'Rouge et Noir' with two gentlemen of those colours cannoning and Noir getting in.

From Whitfield he turned north, up over Knighton Common, back to Tibble's Copse, and then reversed direction to run nearly the same line again, giving a further chance of a cold bath in the brook, which was afforded to another gentleman. Then he headed north, down to Lillington, where the fox somehow mysteriously took himself off and left everyone puzzled, as by no cast could his line be recovered.

The pack then tried Sherborne Park and ran through Lovers' Grove on the line of one who had stolen away into North Wootton Copse. They ran rather well, by Snagharbour Wood, to Haydon, and around to the eastern side of the park. Going through Goathill Wood and around Mews Hill he then went back up the opposite hill, to Deadman's Copse, and towards Windmill Hill as he re-entered Sherborne Park. They lost him in the thick bracken of the Deer Park and left off at about five o'clock after a hard though not brilliant day's work.

GOOD RIDING, AND TWO FOXES, AROUND DEADMOOR COMMON

William W. Connop, at the Manor House, welcomed the Blackmore Vale Hounds to Fifehead Neville on 12 February 1885. He rode again for a while and recalled bygone days when he and Major-General Charles Astell – then in India – were amongst the hardest riders. They found a fox immediately, in Cockrow, which went away like lightening, south-westwards to Locketts Farm and Hazelbury Bryan, where the hounds came to a check, though the fox had been seen in an orchard.

George Orbell cast the hounds and recovered the line. By now he was heading back to Cockrow and they could not mark him in again. Instead they moved on to the wild lands of Deadmoor Common and chopped one there, but could not stay to enjoy it, as two hounds had proceeded to find a line up the hill. Clapping the pack on, Orbell then had the satisfaction of finding and handling his morning fox. He could scarcely travel any further and was run into in the middle of a field.

They then went on over open country to Short Wood, where a good fox took them straight to the withybed at Brockhampton and left for the small covers at Cannings Court, Pulham Rectory, the Halsey Arms, and on to Fir Tree Copse, into which he disappeared. 'Holloas' in all directions provided futile and the run was abandoned after a good 45 minutes. Those who were without second horses were quite relieved.

HARD RIDING REDUCES SEVENTY FIELD TO SEVEN AT TOTNELL CORNER

Some 70 riders gathered beneath the venerable Stockbridge Oak, Lillington, for the Valentine's Day meet of the Blackmore Vale Hounds on 14 February 1885. Lord Haldon (1846–1903) was out, and Mr Weatherby, beside the usual field. They drew the adjoining Little Stockbridge covers, beside the road, and then found in Six Acres. Their fox ran northwards through the gravel pits to Longburton and then turned west to and through Leweston Park. He continued through the wood and into Lillington Wood, then up to Thornford village, where he turned north-east along to Honeycombe Wood, and back-tracked to go to ground on the top of Thornford Hill. It was a gallop of five miles in 35 minutes.

Whitfield Woods then provided more than one inhabitant. It ran away over a series of fine pastures and plentiful fences, almost to Yetminster. Then, ringing around, he returned home to Whitfield, through which the hounds hunted him with a glorious crash of music, finally emerging on the Holm Bushes side. Leaving Six Acres to the left he headed south to the back of Holnest Park and then turned westwards, through Sweethills, and swung up to Totnell Corner at Leigh. Then, leaving Castle Plantation to the south, he turned towards Chetnole and went up into the knoll and out again by Seevoir's to Cockeram's Plantation and eventually completed the circuit to Totnell Corner.

By then, after five o'clock, daylight was failing fast. The hounds had been running for 160 minutes since finding in Whitfield Woods. The Master gave the word for home but there were only seven left to hear it.

STREAM TRAINS AT MILBORNE PORT SPOIL A GOOD SCENT

Meeting at White Post Gate, beside the turnpike house north of Sherborne, the Blackmore Vale Hounds soon found a fox on the steep Clatcombe Hill, on 17 February 1885. He ran downwards and northwards and was lost within a mile in the depths of Holway. Corton Gorse then drew blank. Wheatsheaf Gorse followed with a fox who gave them the trouble of climbing and sliding over Corton Hill, merely to disappear at the bottom.

Back again on Wheatsheaf Hill, three foxes were on foot above Corton Denham, and the dog hounds settled their noses down to one, rattling him in circles around the gorse. 'Who-whoop' proclaimed his retirement to the safe shelter of the main earths, which had been inadvertently left open to receive him. A long walk then proceeded to draw Poyntington Withybed, Milborne Slates, and Vartenham Hill.

After some of the field departed for home, there was a 'view holloa' from Tom, on viewing a brace breaking away from the little cover on Combe Hill. They went away straight as a line, southwards to Crackmore Rocks, across the Pinford end of Sherborne Park, to Goathill. There they turned sharply, north-eastwards through the entire length of Hanover Wood, to cross the Sherborne-Shaftesbury road at Crendle and then follow the hanging woods of East Hill and Everlanes.

Here, reduced to one, he made a sharp turn to the west, with Milborne Port Station and the embankment of the Salisbury-Exeter railway to the north. Having run merrily for five or six fields the hounds suddenly threw up their heads beside the Milborne stream where George Orbell cast forward in vain, after six miles. Railway trains make excellent cover hacks. The time being nearly half past five it was fairly time to stop.

THIRD FOX SAVES HIS BRUSH IN AN HOUR'S CIRCUIT OF NYLAND

Meeting at Buckhorn Weston on 19 February 1885, the Blackmore Vale Hounds drew Langham and Sandley, towards Gillingham. Their first fox was chopped in the turnips and a second took them back to Buckhorn Weston where he was killed in a garden opposite the parish church.

They then turned south, down the vale of the River Cale to Nyland Withybed, where a fox bolted for Lower Nyland and saved himself by rousing his family. The pack went after another, on a fair holding scent, across the Bow Brook and south to Syles Farm and a short check at Henstridge Marsh. He had gone back to Syles and re-crossed the stream, causing more wet coats and wet horses, to the home in Higher Nyland where he was saved by the failing light after providing a pleasing final hour's sport.

EIGHT-MILE ESCAPE, FROM THE KENNELS TO TRENT BARROW

The Kennels meet of the Blackmore Vale Hounds, at Charlton Horethorne, on 28 February 1885, was treated to a bright day and a rising barometer. They cheerfully dashed off after their fox from Thomas Marriott-Dodington's lower cover, over Stowell Hill and Martin's Wood, pointing for Templecombe Station, but then swung up through the North Woods for Cheriton Wood.

A fresh fox jumped up in an orchard and the hounds transferred to him. They ran him sharply through Mr Dodington's park at Horsington, to Templecombe Wood and West Wood, then to the cover at Inwood. They ran him around it and then killed him at the lower end.

They had reached Charlton Wood before finding an undisturbed fox. He went for Cheriton Wood and then swung down to the flat below the Kennels, over ploughed fields to Bristol Gorse, and fairly raced to Sigwells. Swinging sharp to the south-west he went over Corton Beacon and passed below Corton Gorse for Weathergrow and Rimpton. Here, at the first real check after 45 minutes, there was only a faint line. Despite a 'holloa' on Adber Hill, nothing could be done beyond Trent Barrow, after eight miles. One little fox, like many another, had the best of the field, 17 couple of hounds, and all the wisdom and science of Master and men.

Old fox from the Vale eaten on the hills

The Blackmore Vale Hounds met at Chetnole on 2 March 1885 and drew the Knoll and Seiver's Copse before finding in Calfhay Plantation. They went through Cockeram's Plantation on a fair holding scent, to Hilfield and Batcombe, where they rose the hill and ran nicely by and into East Coppice. He went out along the hanging to Up Cerne Wood and White Barn to a smart ring in Cerne Park Wood.

He had been pointing for the Tucking Mill below the Cerne Giant but turned back and over the hill to Sydling Clappers. Still he gave them no rest and revisited Cerne Park, moving on to Elston Hill, and then back again.

They had a check and feared they were going to lose him, but a timely 'holloa' put them right again and they worked the line north to Up Cerne Wood. Here he was viewed and by the time he reached the low end of the cover on the Minterne side of the hill the hounds were ready for him. It was after a circuitous and repetitive eight or nine miles, taking 183 minutes, that they joyfully devoured their prey. He was a big old yellow fox. Rarely, indeed, do hounds from the Vale run up on to those hills to kill and eat one there!

Rain washes out the scent at Lydlinch and Stalbridge

Having met in the rain at Warr Bridge, near Lydlinch, on 3 March 1885, the Blackmore Vale Hounds had their first find in Stock Wood. He made the usual turn through Brickles Wood, which generally throws out the field though not the hounds, and went by Hollow Hill almost to the meet but then turned eastwards to cross the pastures to Lydlinch.

Having crossed the River Lydden, just short of the village, he made for Bagber Gorse, turned at Cook's Farm, and re-crossed the river to the orchard behind the Three Boars' Heads in 40 minutes. Up to here the scent was good but the line back to Brickles Wood was weak and faint.

The pack then went through Thornhill Wood, to the Obelisk Cover, in vain. They later found their customer from the morning at Holtham Plantation, and sent him north through Sturt Plantation and Stalbridge Weston to Stalbridge Park, by which time the rain had washed out what scent there was.

DOUBLE ESCAPES AFTER GOOD RIDES NEAR MAPPOWDER

The meet of the Blackmore Vale Hounds at Barnes Cross on 7 March 1885 soon found in Holwell Plantation. They raced away to the New Inn (Halsey Arms), Pulham, and on under Castle Hill, over Duntish Common to Brockhampton Coppice, to cover three miles in just 14 minutes. Here he was lost but he had provided as pretty a gallop as had been enjoyed for some time. It was enough for a good many of those who had not the luck to have second horses out.

The hounds then made an immediate find on reaching Short Wood, the reliable cover near Mappowder, and ran back to Brockhampton. Turning south their fox made a large loop into the hills in the direction of Plush and was run into a little cover, where they thought they had him, after five miles in 45 minutes. The hounds richly deserved him but somehow their second customer of the day also gave them the slip and had returned to the Blackmore Vale, sinking through the big woods, leaving a declining scent that returned them to Mappowder.

THREE M.F.H.s BUT JUST ONE FOX, AT CAUNDLE MARSH

Meeting at Henry H. Huddleston's picturesque Manor House at Purse Caundle, on 10 March 1885, the Blackmore Vale Hounds drew the small covers behind Ven House, Milborne Port. They did not find until they reached Crendle and then ran their fox, slowly, back to Purse Caundle and Dales Covert.

Having lost here, they found another in Wood House Covert, and made for Plumley Wood and Holt Woods, to Caundle Marsh in a couple of miles. Here they killed their fox in the Brickfields and ate him after 32 minutes.

Their next find was in Haydon Gorse, taking them across Sherborne Park and up to North Wootton Lodge, beyond which the scent failed in Green Lane. The fourth fox of the day jumped up in a wheat field near Snagharbour Wood and was followed northwards to Alweston. He was followed around the place but even the presence of three Masters of Fox Hounds (their own plus Lord Haldon and Colonel Buchannan, the Master of the Lanark and Renfrew) could not improve the scent.

SEVERAL FALLS AND A CONFUSION OF FOXES, ENDING IN BRICKLES WOOD

Having met at Bagber on 12 March 1885, the Blackmore Vale Hounds found a fox near Twin Woods and ran a ring by Robert Rideout Harvey's home at Marnhull. It ran towards Walton Elm and was lost.

From here they went to Yardgrove and found in the hanging wood above the River Stour, making off southwards to Twinwood Coppice. This one was also lost after some falls and muddy coats. Having tried Queen's Copse and found it blank, they moved on to Bagber Gorse, where a hound spoke to a fox in its thick recesses after a long draw. Another was 'holloaed' but these came to nothing.

Having moved into Common Plantation, on Stalbridge Common, they found a fox. He stayed some time in the cover before going away at a sharp angle for Drakes, near which George Orbell and his horse took a different view of a brook, and his stirrup leather went off in a third direction. As the Master held the hounds on, they went on smartly past Jericho, and west of Thornhill Copse as they bore on southwards to Warr Bridge and Lydlinch Common.

The huntsman, George Orbell, rejoined them as they turned west to Stroud Farm, and ran into Stock Wood after three miles and 35 minutes. Their fox was viewed in Brickles Wood, dead-beat, but the hounds divided and a fresh fox saved the old one's life as it approached the time for going home.

FOUR FOXES GIVE THE SLIP AROUND HOLWELL

A large field gathered for the Blackmore Vale Hounds at the Green Man, King's Stag, on 14 March 1885. Finding half a mile to the south, in Pulham Gorse, they galloped to Ponting's Gorse, but then stood still in Holwell Gorse where plenty of foxes had left insufficient scent to press them.

The hounds were working admirably and did better in Holwell Plantation, running their second fox out towards Butterwick Wood, but he turned around just short of it. They ran really well to Buckshaw House and then more slowly to Warry's Plantation, looping back to Holwell Plantation in 45 minutes.

Here a fresh fox got us, and this third subject saved his friend or relative, and himself in the process. Having then drawn New Gorse and Rodmore Plantation blank, they found their fourth in Laines Plantation, Bishop's Caundle, but her timely discretion took her to ground at Mr Spicer's, westwards towards the village, where she was left in safety.

DIVIDED FIELD FROM THORNFORD TO MELBURY BUBB

A large field, including Lord Guilford and Lord Onslow, met the Blackmore Vale Hounds in Thornford village on 23 March 1885. They went straight to Whitfield Woods and found, with a fox going gamely for Tipples, but he then turned and went back through Whitfield to the Holm Bushes, Gordon's Gorse, Gallpits, Sweethills Common and Totnell Corner. From here, after 55 minutes, he seemed to have gone for Bide's Gorse but the pack had divided and three or four couple headed south-west with second whip Bob Cotesworth on a line that went up the Knoll at Chetnole and was heading for Melbury Bubb. After a sharp turn to the south the hounds ran into him and killed after four miles in 160 minutes.

It was a reduced field – those without second horses had given up – that followed the Master back to Thornford Hill to draw Ridge Barn and follow a fox over Knighton Gorse, through Whitfield Woods, and pointing for Clifton Wood, but he swung left in a semi-circle that returned to Whitfield and headed west to Tibble's Copse before going slowly back to Whitfield, where the huntsman's horn was heard yet again with its final echo in a dying day.

ROMEO IS RUN OVER BY A TRAIN AT BUCKHORN WESTON

Another large field met the Blackmore Vale Hounds at Five Bridges, Nyland, on 26 March 1885. They were taken straight to Ashley and there was an immediate find, which after a quick scurry, was given short shrift in the nearby quarry. Going back to Fifehead Magdalen they found another in the lower cover but soon lost him. A third was found in the withybed, by Mr Sandford's farm, and took Trill Lane to cross the River Stour into Ashley withybed and then turned sharply southwards into cottage gardens at Marnhull. A long check, recovering a cold line, ran him slowly near Lloyd's Farm and over the river again, to Sayell's Farm, where he was lost.

The fourth fox of the day, from Lady Theodora's Gorse, provided a real race from Whitchurch, at Henstridge, to Higher Nyland and down through Lower Nyland, and on with a good cry, north-eastwards to Tunnel Head at Buckhorn Weston. Just as hounds were crossing the railway a train dashed into them, causing the death of Romeo – a fine old hound – but the others miraculously escaped. The pack went on steadily, by Quarr Hollow, into the garden of Shanks House, Cucklington. He was so beat he could hardly climb the wall but managed to cross two more fields to go to ground near Clinger Farm. The distance was five miles in 56 minutes. He was dug and bolted but found another hole in only 50 yards. Spades then had him on the move, via Cucklington Parsonage, to Bailey Withybed. He should then have been taken, for the third time, but made yet another of the narrowest escapes a fox ever had. For at that moment they were distracted by a fresh fox.

They briefly transferred to their fifth fox of the day, but huntsman George Orbell spotted their hunted one walking along the road and quickly set them after him again, southwards, and back into Dorset at Quarr Hollow. Here he made his fourth and final trick of escapology and was never seen again.

HOUNDS AND FOX END UP IN A TEMPLECOMBE LIVING ROOM

The Sherborne Park meet of the Blackmore Vale Hounds on 28 March 1885, gathering beside Pinford Bridge, headed south to Green Lane and Snagharbour Wood, North Wootton, where they found and killed almost immediately. Their second fox took them back to Pinford Farm and Crackmore Rocks and then turned south-westwards to follow the railway line to Oborne and Castleton. He tried to cross the railway but was headed back to Sherborne Park and entered the ruins of the Old Castle. One hound, Placable, caught him over the gateway – from which he fell – and he then slipped into the adjoining Castle Gardens where he was killed after three miles in 80 minutes.

Other covers were drawn and their third fox was found on Combe Hill, Milborne Port. He raced to the back of the village and there was a short check on cold plough-lands. Having recovered the line they followed him merrily over the little brook to pass to the south of the railway embankment, into Station Covert and at top speed through Thomas Marriott-Dodington's new cover on the side of Everlanes Hill. This fine fox went on through West Wood and straight as a die on to Templecombe, keeping the railway to his left. He then followed the main line into the middle of the village where he jumped over a wall and dashed into the open door of a cottage.

Seventeen couple of furious hounds followed it and filled the small living room to the consternation of an old lady who was sobbing and thought her last hour was come. The Master took the fox from the hounds, to give them a fine worry in the orchard, and the trembling old lady had a story to tell to her dying day. This was a rare dash of four miles in 32 minutes.

RUNNING AROUND DEADMOOR COMMON

William W. Connop's hospitality, at the Manor House, Fifehead Neville, provided an excellent start to the meet of the Blackmore Vale Hounds on 31 March 1885. They disturbed a fox at Cockrow and were led at a pace to Kitford, Woolland Cover, and the chalk escarpment which was reached in 15 minutes. They went on through Stoke Wake, Rawlsbury Camp, and Bulbarrow Hill, then into one of the covers beside Melcombe Park. After a pretty gallop of 47 minutes he doubled back and was lost in the wood.

The hounds returned to Mappowder and had a long trot back to Badbury, where the only tenant was a large cat, and found their second fox on Deadmoor Common. He ran well past Cockrow, on to Hazelbury Common, but was then lost. Back at Deadmoor, there was a 'holloa' almost immediately, revealing a fox in the fields towards Rooksmoor Copse. Orbell gathered up his hounds and galloped to it, through Rooksmoor and Charity Gorse, in a circuit back to Deadmoor Common and over it, by Haydon Gorse, for Stock Wood. He then turned and looped once again, for a final circle around Deadmoor Common, where he was finally killed after a merry run of 55 minutes.

HUMAN DISCRETION SAVES VIXEN IN A CHINA CUPBOARD AT FOLKE

The meet of the Blackmore Vale Hounds on 2 April 1885 should have been listed for Haydon Lodge, beside Sherborne Park, but a typographical error caused it to be advertised as 'Haddon' Lodge, so there were horses and grooms all across the country. Haydon Gorse was drawn blank, followed by Windmill and Ashcombe, but there was a brace of foxes in Ferney Down Wood at Bishop's Down.

Then the hounds took to the one leaving by the lower end of the cover, enabling the horses to avail themselves of Kitford Bridge, and went off via Withy Tree Copse in a not very direct course to Broke and Folke. Here the vixen discreetly retired into a china cupboard in the kitchen at Manor Farm and the huntsman, equally discreetly, left her there, and ushered everyone on from the home of farmer Philip Adams.

They soon found another fox in Marsh Copse, to run nicely over Portdown Hill and ford the Caundle Brook near Poll Bridge. Leaving Ryall Gorse to the north they went on to Major William Warry's home, at Westrow House, and then south into Manor Plantation where they lost the scent.

Having trotted back to Tripps Gorse, their third fox went away with a will, to Haydon Gorse, Ashcombe, and the brickfields at Caundle Marsh. It was all anyone could do to keep the hounds in sight. They doubled round to the woods on Holt Hill and Tut Hill, dropping down to Marsh Court and Caundle Marsh Wood, where he turned sharp and short and was killed instantly after 36 minutes.

NYLAND FOX PROVIDES BEST RUN OF THE SEASON

The Master of the Blackmore Vale Hounds met very early at his Inwood home on 4 April 1888, because of Point-to-Point races in the afternoon. He moved off punctually at eight o'clock and drew the hedgerows eastwards down beside Lady Theodora's Gorse to enter

Dorset at Nyland. Here the hounds clapped on to a fox who had been viewed moments before and gave 'a lovely burst of music' as they raced over the pastures beside the River Cale.

They ran through Pelsham Farm, heading for Kington Magna, and then followed the railway line eastwards to Buckhorn Weston Tile Yard where there was a check. Casting themselves beautifully, the hounds were off again on the line and it was all that could be done to keep them in sight as they re-traced their steps to Lower Nyland and then went on to Temple Lane. Their course was now straight, southwards to Derigree, Mohuns Park, and the Shaftesbury-Sherborne road at Bazeland's Hill. He was pointing for Stalbridge and seemed to be making for Prior's Down.

Instead he turned smartly to the north-east and went back across the Sherborne road at Bow Bridge to the final couple of fields towards Nyland. Then there was a noisy 'who-whoop' as the eager pack pulled their prey down in the open after crossing seven miles, to return to within yards of the starting point, in 88 minutes. The cream of the core of the country had been covered at a pace which made everyone feel it had been the run of the season.

In the afternoon the Point-to-Point races took place at Hazlegrove where accidents were rife. Mr Chichester suffered a particularly heavy fall. Sir Elliott Lees M.P., of South Lytchett House, was the winner on Damon.

COLONEL DIGBY FALLS AT SWEETHILLS

The Blackmore Vale Hounds met at the White Horse, Middlemarsh, on 12 April 1888 and had a fine run southwards from Cosmore Common and Eight Acre Coppice, rising the escarpment through Mount Silver and Remedy. He then made westwards for Up Cerne, north towards Batcombe, and then north-eastwards through the hanging woods of Telegraph Hill and High Stoy to return to Remedy where he was lost after a challenging 65 minutes.

They found their second fox in Admiral Digby's Plantation and ran towards Sweethills, approaching which Colonel the Hon. Everard Digby (1852–1914) had a nasty fall, while jumping a stack of timber. Having turned for Holnest House, they crossed the park which was the last home of Mr Drax, squire and sportsman, until he moved into the mock-Byzantine mausoleum he had prepared for himself in 1882, well ahead of his death on 5 January 1887. Their fox went on as if for Berkeley Gorse but then turned for Boys Hill and passed the old Grange House. Having made this distance in a respectable 30 minutes, the pace slowed, and he was marked to ground by Woodfalls, in the main earth just out of Blackmore Vale country. So there he was left.

TREEING A FOX FOR THE MARCHIONESS OF WESTMINSTER

Having reached her ninety-fourth year and moved from Motcombe to Inwood, Elizabeth, the Marchioness of Westminster, was treated to the sight of a fox being tree'd. It had been killed just outside the grounds and her son-in-law, the Master, ordered the huntsman to bring in into view of the windows and place it in a tree so that the Marchioness could watch the final scene. For some time the hounds bayed their fox beautifully and vied with each other in their efforts to dislodge it. There was much excitement when at last they succeeded, in which Lady Westminster took her full share.

The oldest sportswoman in the world, she said it recalled the memories of her youth, when in the second and third decades of the century, while George IV and William IV were on the throne, she had hunted with the Belvoir and Quorn Hounds.

MASTER'S RETIREMENT FOLLOWED BY DISPERSAL OF THE PACK

The double sadness for Thomas Merthyr Guest (1838–1904), having seen out the century in the saddle, was that retirement in May 1900 was followed by the dispersal of the Blackmore Vale Hounds. Having hunted the country at his own expense, he reluctantly resigned the mastership, with the hope that the Hunt Committee would take on the hounds. This was declined and the hundred couple of hounds therefore had to be sold.

The famous Blackmore Vale blood-line, originating with the packs established by Mr Digby and Sir Richard Glyn, had been enriched by Mr Guest's purchases. These had included Bajazet, Lexicon, Oliver, Painter, Vigilant and Villager, with eleven ladies, from the New Forest and Burton sale in 1885 when Mr Meyrick gave up the country. The same year, when T. Harvey Bayly was Master of the Rufford, one of the outcrosses introduced by Mr Guest was Rufford Denmark which sired no less than six couple of the entry to the register in the following year. Among these was Druid (1886), whose dam was Woodbine (1882), a daughter of Mr Garth's Wildfire, with the female line going back to Ruby (1864). Druid was a reliable hound who perfected his own effective method for catching a scent. He would stand on his hind-legs and point his nose high into the air. When that failed he was known to jump, upwards, to optimise his chances.

The five-year-old ladies Gossamer, Willing and Rhetoric came from the Earl of Lonsdale's sale in 1887. Gambler and Gaylad were from the North Warwickshire Hunt, and the ladies Wanton, Restless and Lapwing came from the Burton Hounds, in 1888. Landsman, Trimmer, Regent, Villager, Gannymede and Lecturer were purchased at Mr Harding Cox's sale in 1889. Ransom and the ladies Winifred and Artful were bought in Rugby, from Sir Watkin Wynn, in 1890. Other purchases that year were Ringwood and Miser from the Pytchley Hunt and Solomon, Ferryman and Woodman from Mr Ferne.

In 1891 Mr Guest bought nine hounds from the East Essex and 15 from the South Devon. Weeper was bought from Colonel Garratt in 1892. That year also saw Watchman (1890) – Blackmore Vale born and sold – and Watkin arrive with the young ladies Priceless and Prudence from C.D. Seymour, the Master of the West Norfolk Hounds. In Watchman, Mr Guest had bought back a remarkably independent hound, who would make his own cast right round a field, and then speak with such confidence on finding the line that the whole pack would respond and join him. Watchman was by Ancaster (1887) with Wrekin (1885). Ancaster was the son of Newsman, from Oakley, and through his dam Amabel (1881) strained back through Russian (1871) to Belvoir Guider and the Commodore-Matchless family.

Also in 1892, the two-year-olds Ravish, a lady, and Freedom, arrived from the Atherstone Hounds. Blackmore Vale-born Rama and her brother Raleigh (1894) proved to be highly individualistic hounds, with Rama refusing to go home with the pack and sneaking back to the Inwood kennels in her own time. She was an inveterate cat-hunter, as was Raleigh, who was fond of making a diversion through cottage gardens and woe betide the domestic pussy who was not quick enough to save herself in the nearest apple-tree. Raleigh and Comrade would always give a personal welcome to the Master with their own short, sharp bark, when he joined the hounds at a meet. These are just a few vignettes to give an indication of the life and times of the hounds that made the Blackmore Vale story possible. They also show Mr Guest's popularity with the animals in his care which corresponded to the admiration he won from farmers for protecting the interests of those who worked the land they crossed.

His final significant purchase, in 1896, was the acquisition of the celebrated Brocklesby Dogs from Lord Lonsdale. With this line he was able to start uniting just about all known strains of foxhound blood. The Blackmore Vale Hounds had now achieved an equal fame which would be reflected in their dispersal over England, France and America.

There was no official testimonial to Mr Guest – though he had been offered 'a choice between plate and picture' – but that was down to the national situation rather than hurt feelings. He declined because of the Boer War in South Africa, creating 'the present inauspicious moment, when every man's purse is being called upon to assist the resources of the Empire.' His devoted adherents decided otherwise, however, with 800 mustering at the Master's home at Inwood on 26 April 1900 for a presentation to the Master and Lady Theodora. Most were farmers. Even more gathered for the meet which followed at noon – with a record field numbering in excess of a thousand – and swarmed into the Blackmore Vale in a sight never equalled before or since.

Left: Blackmore Vale and Sparkford huntsman of 1995, on Windmill Hill at Yenston, on the former Inwood Estate of the Victorian Master, Merthyr Guest.

Above: Return visit, 150 years later, to Holbrook House, at the invitation of Geoffrey and Joan Taylor, for a special meet where Henry Hall, in 1831, had founded one of the gentleman hunts that would become the Blackmore Vale Hounds.

Right: Setting off, via the A371, as the Blackmore Vale Hounds move out from the commemorative meet at Holbrook House, in 1981.

Fox in flight, from the Blackmore Vale Hounds.

Orphaned cub, rescued by a
follower of the Blackmore Vale.

First find of the day, as a fox breaks from cover, for the Blackmore Vale Hounds.

Ready for action, on arrival at a Blackmore Vale meet.

Droveway photo-call, in a typically wet green lane, for the Blackmore Vale Hounds near
Sturminster Newton, seen from a bridge on the Somerset and Dorset Railway.

Classroom view, looking down on a Blackmore Vale meet in
The Courts at Sherborne School, circa 1972.

Arable watch, for the Blackmore Vale, near Stalbridge in the 1960s.

Hound show, for prize members of the Blackmore Vale, in 1975.

Huckworthy Basset Hounds at the Blackmore Vale Kennels,
Charlton Horethorne, in 1976.

Check for the Blackmore Vale, on a rise above the River Lydden, near Lydlinch.

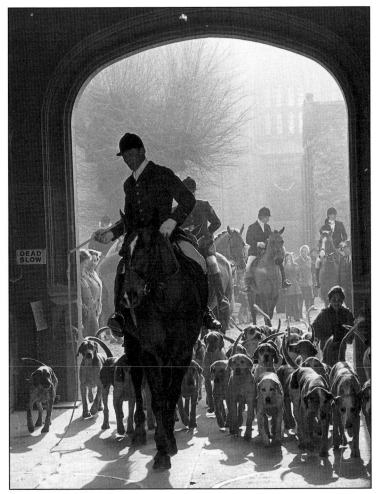

Setting off from Sherborne School with the Blackmore Vale in 1975.

Break out – a good runner is off, leading the Blackmore Vale pack.

Following field, with the Blackmore Vale crossing a chalkland ridge near Batcombe.

Hill country, which rises for the Blackmore Vale from Bulbarrow to the Dorsetshire Gap.

Setting off, with the Blackmore Vale, deep in their home country.

The Blackmore Vale pack, out for exercise in a lane near Sherborne, in the 1960s.

A meet of the Blackmore Vale in The Courts of Sherborne School in about 1972.

Blackmore Vale country, seen from the downland escarpment, in the 1960s.

Chapter Twelve

THE RANSTON BLOODHOUNDS

OUT WITH LORD WOLVERTON

 The 3rd Baron Wolverton (who died in 1888) was the Master of the Ranston Bloodhounds which he established from young hounds bought in 1871 and had by 1875 worked-up into a pack of sixteen and a half couple, mainly of his own breeding, with which he hunted carted deer in the Blackmore Vale for eight seasons. The bloodhounds stood 27 or 28 inches and were direct descendants of the old black St Huberts – making them a genuine hound of pure blood – of the type that hunted Blackmore Forest and Cranborne Chase in the early Middle Ages. Major Whyte-Melville recorded that 'their limbs and frame were proportioned to so gigantic a stature' with rounded feet and 'powerful legs symmetrically straight'. Having their origins in the dense forests of the Ardennes they hunted entirely by scent and never raised their heads for a view of the quarry.

They were based at Ranston House, Shroton, and met at Hayes for what Alys F. Serrell, on Countess, cherished as 'one of the best 45 minutes I have ever had in the Vale'. In the company of Lady Theodora Grosvenor (as she was before her marriage to Merthyr Guest), on Mars, she looked back on 'a lovely spring day' – 8 April, to be more precise, early in the Seventies – with the Master and men appearing in a smart uniform of green coat with gilt buttons. These had a coronet with the letter 'W'. The field included Major Whyte-Melville; Captain Paget of the 7th Hussars; Captain the Hon. Alfred Byng, also of the 7th Hussars; Major Ness; Captain Brown; Digby Collins; Walter Grove and Mr H. Harris, acting as pilot to Lady Theodora.

They proceeded to sweep along 'like a whirlwind' after the good deer (Lady Wolverton, as it was nicknamed) was uncarted beside Rossiter's Farm. More than one good horse refused big double fences towards the Marnhull road. The Master and most of the field were thrown out by a sharp turn at Andrew's Farm and a similar change of direction at Margaret Marsh saw Major Ness rolling over by an open trench. Fences then came thick and fast, in a steeplechase following the hounds, which were only 20 yards behind the hind. The chase followed over the road from Todber to Marnhull and passed Nash Covert to the new bridge over the River Stour.

Lady Theodora and Mr Harris were across the water when they saw that the deer was on the other side. Harris and Digby Collins rolled over in the mud. The hounds had carried on northwards for the lower Fifehead coverts and Five Bridges where they were entirely at a loss. Beyond, at Nyland, Lord Wolverton eventually joined Lady Theodora and Miss Serrell. He had been riding the roads trying to find his hounds, and had gathered up the two Hussars and Captain Brown, but the attempts at a cast would prove useless. They had news of her reaching Kington Magna but no line could be found in two hours of searching. The wonderful career of Lady Wolverton resumed at 4.30 pm when the Master eventually found her at Kington and ran her for 40 minutes to an out-house near Wincanton. It was nine o'clock that night before Lord Wolverton reached home.

Sixteen-mile run, from Buckhorn Weston to Stoke Wake

On 7 March 1874, the Ranston Bloodhounds met at Fifehead Magdalen, to look for a hind that had been feeding with the cows on Loder's Farm at Buckhorn Weston. This deer had given a capital 40 minutes, from Manston, the week before and had been lost at Rodgrove, towards Wincanton.

The chase resumed across open-trenched fields and stiff fences from Loder's Farm to Rodgrove and then eastwards to Shanks Farm, Cucklington, and Langham, at Gillingham. Here the hounds recovered the line and bore down to the South-Western Railway, passing under the arch, and went round to Eccliffe Mill with the river in front. The hounds and field crossed by the deep ford and made fairly straight for Stour Provost and then south of Todber to the River Stour between Marnhull and Hinton St Mary. The field crossed a narrow plank bridge at Cut Mill to Pentridge Farm and the Somerset and Dorset Railway.

The pace slowed, not helped by double hedges, and the hind was viewed in a branch of the River Divelish between Bagber Bridge and the railway line at Blackwater Bridge. The field, by now reduced from a hundred to fifteen, went on southwards to Bagber Brickfields and Haydon Common to Stoke Wake, where she was taken after a run of 16 miles – much of it at racing pace – in 150 minutes. Lady Theodora Grosvenor and Mrs Clay Ker Seymer were well up till near the end. The only members of the field who were still at the front were Merthyr Guest, Mr Clay Ker Seymer and one of the whippers-in. There had been a good deal of grief on the way; it was rumoured that a tree had to be cut down in order to free (Sir) Walter Grove from his predicament.

TWO HINDS REFUSE TO RUN FROM MANSTON

A fair-sized field met Lord Wolverton and nine couple of the Ranston Bloodhounds at Manston in March 1874. Among them were Major Whyte-Melville, Mr and Mrs Clay Ker Seymer, Lady Theodora Grosvenor, Captain Robin Coote from Weymouth and Captain Henry Bridges of Fifehead House, Fifehead Magdalen. The deer was uncarted and trotted off in a lackadaisical manner into a little covert where she was eventually persuaded to leave her refuge but proceeded to return from where she came. The hind was secured, returned to the cart, and another released.

This set off at a pace with the hounds making magnificent music but only for some half-dozen fields before she was surrounded by the bloodhounds. She was separated and given another chance to run away but sank into a pond and refused to play the game any more. So ended a day of failures.

Other runs were very different, with one red deer stag going straight as a die to the north-west and not being seen for the rest of the day, with news coming a week later that he was grazing at Wells beside the Mendip Hills. The reason turned out to have been his experience in the cart when the driver stopped for a drink at the Ship in West Stour. The deer-cart ran away at what witness G.B. Starky described as '100 miles an hour' and though later secured and brought to the meet the experience had just about frightened the poor deer to death.

Lord Wolverton kept the mastership of the bloodhound pack until 1880 when he sold them to Lord Carrington and subsequently hunted the country around Shroton with harriers.

Chapter Thirteen

MISS SERRELL'S OTTER HOUNDS

OTTERS AT LYDLINCH AND HOLWELL

 Miss Alys F. Serrell's Otter Hounds, a pack of terriers, accounted for their first otter when they met at Twofords Bridge, Lydlinch, on 7 May 1889. They drew the River Lydden upstream to Perry Farm where Nettle found an otter in a drain that opened down into the water. When the otter tried to bolt the crowd on the opposite bank shouted and the sent him back on the terrier. Nettle was pulled out and Racer let in, which had the otter facing the entrance, as the two hounds collared another otter instantly.

A week later they started from King's Stag and found a brace of otters at Hazelbury Mill. The terriers divided, with two couple following a vixen upstream, while the rest of the pack turned downstream after the other. The terriers that were after the vixen were Sharper, Amber, Nettle and Jubilee. Several times they forced their quarry to try to land, which she eventually did about a mile from the start, and then made a dash for open land back towards the mill. Sharper was close on her, caught a view, and rolled her over. The other terriers were on his heels as they had her, without any assistance, though Amber was badly bitten through the throat.

Miss Serrell returned to the main pack to find demoralised little dogs and incessant shouting from the field. She rallied the former and went on to account for a dog-otter in an hour. The earlier kill had been recovered in reasonable condition, turning the scales at 18 pounds, and would be stuffed and mounted in a glass case.

Their largest specimen was found on the Cam at Buckshaw House, Holwell, on 14 April 1893. Sharper had marked him to ground near the mill-pond and a spade soon had him bolting fast and furious. The terriers had a fine hunt through unpleasantly cold waters before he took refuge in the stump of a river-bank tree. Little Floss, Miss Serrell's house pet, let herself down from the top and managed to hang on to the otter's head, until Amber and the other terriers

169

could reach them. The keeper then succeeded in taking the otter and hauling him up, for a 'who-whoop' to be sounded as the whole pack swarmed around him. The otter was described as 'a fine fellow of 24 pounds'.

Later in the month, having met at Pulham, the pack of seven and half couple found an otter in the stream above Hazelbury Bryan. Three terriers – Royal, Amber and Nettle – nailed the otter under a stump and killed him in the water as the whole pack went in for a grand worry, with half-drowned terriers still clinging to the dead otter.

Meanwhile, a little black-and-tan named Bugle had lost her footing, and appeared in front of the bank-side field who mistook her for the otter and proceeded to beat her with sticks. 'It's the dog, you fools!' cried William Connop, waving his stick, as he came to the rescue. It was one of the last active days with her own pack for Miss Serrell who parted with her country to Mr Courtenay Tracy in 1894.

Otter hounds bound for the River Wey, from a 1930s meet of the Culmstock Otterhounds, beneath the railway bridge at Broadwey.

A cheerful looking meet of the Seavington at Broadoak, near Symondsbury, circa 1965.

Hunting on foot, with a very level pack of the Down House Beagles, at a 1920s lawn meet at Chilfrome.

Culmstock Otterhounds moving off, down the River Piddle.
The setting is near Piddlehinton in the mid-1930s.

Splashing time as the Culmstock Otterhounds draw the weedy shallows
of the River Piddle near Briantspuddle, in about 1935.

'Mark well the wanton females of thy pack
That curl their taper tails, and freaking court
Their piebald mates enamoured; their red eyes
Flash fires improve; nor rest, nor food they take,
Goaded by furious love.'

- Peter Beckford

INDEX

Abbotsbury 21, 24, 26, 27, 99, 101, 111, 118
Adams, Philip 152
Adber 141, 146
Admiston 36, 86, 88, 92, 94
Affpuddle 76, 86, 94, 95
Allen, George 142
Alington, Lord 45, 87
Almer 81, 96
Alton Pancras 32, 35, 39, 40, 50, 92, 132
Alweston 139, 148
Anderson 15, 22, 34
Anderson, Dick 129
Ansty 29, 30, 35, 43, 61, 64, 67, 71, 80, 92
Armswell 19, 32, 39, 40, 43, 60, 85-87, 92, 132
Askerswell 27, 28, 28, 46
Astell, Charles 144
Athelhampton 36, 39, 41, 88
Atkinson, Kit 66, 67, 96

Bagber [Milton Abbas] 30, 37, 77, 81, 88, 89, 93, 94, 95, 103
Bagber [Sturminster Newton] 23, 59, 68, 133, 136-138, 143, 149, 167
Baker, Solomon 20, 50
Balston, Mr 57
Bampfylde, Augustus Frederick George Warwick 99
Bankes, family 31
Baring, Francis 137
Barnes, William 105
Barrow 139
Batcombe [Dorset] 23, 35, 41, 62, 92, 147, 162
Batcombe [Somerset] 54
Bayford 142
Bayly, T. Harvey 154
Beckford, Julines 9
Beckford, Peter 6, 8-11, 13, 14, 70, 173
Bedford, Duke of 22
Beer Hacket 143
Belchalwell 43
Bentinck, Cavendish 142
Bere Regis 15, 22, 27, 29, 45, 58, 69, 75-77, 81, 83, 84, 87, 90, 94-96, 98
Berkeley, Edward 66
Berkeley, William Henry 67, 71, 84
Bexington 26, 27, 99, 101
Bingham, Lord 37
Bingham's Melcombe 30, 62, 63, 65, 71, 80, 89, 91, 92

Bincombe 91
Binnegar 84
Bishop's Caundle 18, 19, 39, 54, 68, 89, 143, 149
Blackmore Vale 18, 21, 31, 32, 39, 40, 54, 56, 58, 60, 61, 63, 68, 69, 74, 89, 102, 129-166
Blackmore Vale Hounds 129-166
Blandford 12, 15, 18-20, 29, 36, 37, 41, 44, 45, 69, 82, 84
Blandford St Mary 44
Bloxworth 69, 81, 83, 84, 96, 97
Bockhampton 57
Bournemouth 78
Boveridge 19
Bowden 137
Bovington 26, 85, 87
Bradford Abbas 142
Bradford Peverell 19, 21, 29, 33, 46, 82, 83, 111, 112
Bradney, John 142
Briantspuddle 27, 60, 76, 83, 86, 87, 94, 95, 172
Bridge, Mr 40
Bridges, Henry 168
Bridehead 21, 24, 27, 42, 82, 100, 101
Bridport 18-21, 25-29, 32, 42, 46, 86, 100
Brine, James 36
Broad Chalke 18, 20
Broadmayne 57, 91, 106
Broadoak 171
Broadwey 24, 104, 171
Broadwindsor 27
Brockhampton 144, 148
Brown, Captain 166, 167
Brownsea Island 142
Bruton 54
Bryanston 15, 36, 39, 46, 66, 68, 70, 129
Brymer, John 142
Brymer, William Ernest 88, 95, 142
Buchannan, Colonel 148
Buckhorn Weston 134, 141, 142, 150, 153, 167
Buckland Newton 19, 31, 32, 40, 41, 57, 60, 62, 67, 92
Buckland Ripers 19, 21, 24-26, 83, 99
Buckshaw 89, 134, 136, 139, 149, 169
Bullen, Tatchel 24
Burgess, family 15, 70, 77
Burleston 38, 39, 84
Burtenshaw, whip 103
Burton [Charminster] 32, 76, 100

Burton [Wool] 26
Burton Bradstock 28
Butler, Rev William 'Billy' 16, 24, 89
Byng, Alfred 166

Cain, Betsy 93
Caines, James 36
Came 38, 59, 90
Canford 86
Cannings Court 67, 89, 93, 144
Castleton 151
Cattistock 19, 25, 27, 29, 32, 36, 49, 99-103, 107-128
Caundle Marsh 18, 19, 39, 54, 68, 69, 136, 143, 148, 152
Cave, R. 95
Cerne Abbas 19, 20, 23, 30, 32, 35, 40, 41, 42, 59, 67, 88, 93, 96, 102, 147
Chadwick, Edward 142
Chafyn-Grove, William 8
Chalbury 31
Channing, John 54
Chaldon Herring 18, 30, 90
Charborough 60, 64, 66, 74-79, 81, 129, 134
Charlton Horethorne 130, 137, 146, 160
Charminster 32, 45, 100, 118, 119
Cheselbourne 29, 30, 35, 36, 37, 41, 44, 67, 76, 77, 81, 89, 92, 103, 132
Cheriton 146
Chetnole 19, 63, 142, 145, 147, 150
Chetwynd, Georgina and Sir George 101
Chichester, Charles 142
Chickerell 19, 21, 24, 25, 83, 99
Chilcombe 19, 27, 28
Chilfrome 116, 171
Child Okeford 70, 103, 142
Clayton, Mr and Mrs 134, 142
Clifton Maybank 19, 44
Clyffe 15, 26
Codrington, Mr 46, 101
Coker's Frome 33, 45, 76
Collins, Digby 140, 166, 167
Compton Pauncefoot 54, 142
Compton Valence 19, 42, 46, 100
Connop, William W. 142, 144, 151, 170
Coote, Robin 168
Corscombe 102
Corton 83
Corton Denham 145, 146
Coryates 108, 115

Cox, Harding 154
Cranborne 9, 10, 19, 40, 45, 68, 71, 89, 166
Crane, Mr 27, 92
Creech Grange 79
Crewkerne 20
Crendle 146, 148
Crichel 15-17, 19, 31, 40, 44, 73, 89
Cucklington 133, 141, 150
Culmstock Otter Hounds 171, 172
Curry Rivel 142

Dale, Charles William 102
Damer, G. L. D. 65
Damer, Mr 64
Davis, Edward 77
Davis, James 40, 41
Davis, M. 56
Davis, Samuel 30, 35
Delcombe 43, 45, 64, 67, 70, 87, 93
Dendy, Arthur 133
Dendy, Samuel 132
Dewlish 15, 19, 29, 30, 35, 41, 44, 58, 71, 76, 77, 80, 81, 84, 85, 88, 90, 93, 95, 96, 103, 132
Digby, E. H. T. 102
Digby, Everard 153
Digby, H. 63
Digby, Lord 41, 68, 96, 136
Digby, George Wingfield 89, 129, 130, 132, 154
Ditcheat 142
Donhead St Andrew 20
Donniscombe, John 66, 70
Dorchester 15, 19-22, 24, 25, 27-29, 32, 33, 35, 37, 38, 42-46, 57, 69, 76, 82, 83, 86, 91, 95, 101, 103, 105, 116-118
Dorchester, Lord 10
Down House 43, 44, 81
Down House Beagles 171
Drake, Mr 129
Drax, John Samuel Wanley Sawbridge Erle 60, 66, 74-79, 83, 97, 129, 130, 134, 153
Druce 35, 36, 39, 41, 45, 67, 76, 84, 85, 88, 93, 95, 96, 100, 103
Dugdale, Major 142
Duncliffe 69
Dungarvan, Viscount 129
Duntish 30, 31, 33, 34, 35, 92, 93, 102, 138, 139, 148
Durweston 45, 56, 70

East Chinnock 18
East Knowle 18, 19
Eastbury 15, 18, 19, 24, 25, 27, 29, 32, 38, 40, 41
Edward, Prince of Wales [Edward VIII] 130
Edwards, Lionel 12
Erichson, Professor 102
Erle-Drax-Grosvenor, Jane 74
Eton College Beagles 128

Evans, John 99, 101
Evershot 120
Fabian Society 136
Farquharson, Frederick Thomas 18, 26
Farquharson, James John 10, 11, 18-53, 76, 80, 82, 83, 129, 130
Ferne 19
Ferne, Mr 155
Fetherstonhaugh-Frampton, Harry Rupert 103
Fiddleford 137
Fifehead Neville 19, 23, 32, 36, 43, 58, 142, 151
Fifehead Magdalen 23, 131, 140, 144, 150, 167, 168
Fitzroy, Robert O'Brien 95
Fleet 26, 83, 99
Floyer, John 26, 33
Folke 18, 134, 139, 152
Fontmell Parva 133
Fookes, Henry 93
Fookes, Robert 34
Fookes, William 93, 103
Forbes, Hamilton 142
Fordington 21, 38
Forston 30-33, 99
Frampton 16, 21, 23, 28, 29, 30, 42, 46, 99, 115
Friar Waddon 27, 83, 90, 91
Friarmayne 91
Frome 54
Frome St Quintin 114
Fyler, Mr 60

Galton, John 74
Garratt, Colonel 155
George, Prince Regent 16
Gillingham 18, 129, 133, 134, 146, 167
Glanvilles Wootton 19, 21, 32, 102, 139, 140
Glyn, Captain 92
Glyn, Sir Julius 131, 141
Glyn, Sir Richard 71, 130, 131, 133, 141, 154
Goathill 135, 144, 145
Godmanstone 19, 23, 42, 115
Gooden, John 142
Goodenough, Mr 23
Godwin, Mr 70
Gorwell 24, 25, 27, 82, 101
Graham, Mr 30
Grant, Sir Colquhoun 29
Grant, Sir Francis 46, 47
Grant-Dalton, Dalton Foster 133, 142
Grimstone 21, 23, 30, 41, 42, 122, 123
Grissell, Captain 142
Grosvenor, Lady Elizabeth 154
Grosvenor, Lady Theodora 131, 166-168
Grove, Sir Walter 166, 167
Guest, Lady Theodora 7, 131, 134, 135, 141, 143, 150, 152, 155
Guest, Monty 86

Guest, Thomas Merthyr 131, 132, 134-138, 141, 154, 166
Guilford, Earl 101-103, 149
Gundry, Joseph Pearkes Fox 86, 103
Gussage All Saints 19, 71

Haldon, Lord 144
Hall, Henry 24, 46, 66, 129, 156
Hampreston 142
Hamworthy 82
Hambro, Charles Joseph Theophilus 86, 96
Hankey, Montagu 103
Hanford 70
Harbin, Major 142
Harding, James 33, 57, 63, 65
Hardy Monument 21, 25, 27, 82, 101, 114
Hardy, Thomas 105
Harris, H. 166, 167
Hart, Mr 22
Hartfoot Lane 61-63, 65, 91
Harvey, Richard Rideout 148
Haydon 135, 139, 144, 148, 152
Hazelbury Bryan 32, 36, 43, 58, 65, 91, 152, 169, 170
Hazlegrove 153
Hector's Brewery 37
Henbury 82
Henstridge 131, 134, 140, 141, 150
Hermitage 61, 135
Hethfelton 60, 85, 86
Hilfield 34, 41, 61, 62, 93, 140, 147
Hilton 37, 43, 64, 65, 80
Hinton Martell 130, 141
Hinton St Mary 136, 137, 167
Holbrook 129, 156
Holford, Thomas 102
Holnest 21, 61, 63, 134, 140, 145, 153
Holton 132
Holwell 32, 89, 132, 134, 149, 169
Holway 141, 145
Holworth 90
Holywell 35
Homer, Mr 84
Honey, Harry 76
Hooke 27, 28, 100
Horsington 146
Horton 32
House, family 15, 22, 34, 40, 70, 77
Huckworthy Basset Hounds 168
Huddleston, Henry H. 148
Hull, William Shetler 95
Hunt Servants' Benefit Society 97, 131
Hurst 58
Hussey, Giles 142
Hutchings, Eliza 27
Hyde 60, 70, 80, 84, 86, 98

Ibberton 39, 43, 45, 56, 70, 87
Ilchester, Earl of 30, 32, 33, 45, 63, 88, 99-101
Ilsington 27, 38, 41, 88, 92, 94, 95, 142

Inwood 131, 134, 135, 141, 146, 152, 154-156
Iwerne Stepleton 9-12, 18

Jennings, Ben 20, 22, 23, 26, 32, 47, 51, 89
Jordan, Tom 142

Kennett, George 84, 85, 87
Kent, Mr 81
Kerr, Dr 102
Kerslake, Mr 58
King's Stag 32, 36, 43, 62, 67, 68, 132, 133, 143, 149, 169
Kingston Lacy 20, 82
Kingston Maurward 32, 33, 57
Kingston Russell 20-22, 24, 25, 27-29, 42, 82, 100
Kington Magna 140, 153, 167
Knighton 143, 144

Langden, Sir Godfrey 142
Langdon, Churchill 131
Langham 134, 146, 147, 167
Langton Herring 26, 83, 99, 108
Langton Long Blandford 18, 49
Last, John 76
Lees, Sir Elliott 155
Leigh 41, 61, 63, 137, 145
Leir, William Marriott 142
Leweston 21, 34, 61, 138
Lillington 19, 34, 138, 144, 145
Little, Harry 86
Littlebredy 21, 22, 24, 100, 101
Litton Cheney 28, 29, 46, 82, 100
Loftus, Captain 62, 63, 65
Long Bredy 27, 29, 82, 100
Long Crichel 20, 31
Long, Dr 131
Long, Walter 136
Longburton 20, 134, 145
Longman's Stables 35
Longleat 54, 129
Lonsdale, Earl of 154, 155
Lovelace, James 96
Luttrell, Alexander Fownes 135, 142
Luttrell, John 133
Lydlinch 18, 19, 43, 54, 58, 59, 62, 67, 68, 129, 137, 147, 149, 160, 169
Lytchett Matravers 64, 69, 81
Lytchett Minster 153

Maiden Newton 19, 20, 28, 30, 116, 124
Manley, Miss 86
Mansel-Pleydell, Edmund 10, 56
Manston 133, 136, 167
Mappowder 20, 34, 36, 58, 60, 67, 85, 89, 91, 92, 94, 132, 148, 151
Margaret Marsh 69, 166
Marnhull 23, 69, 133, 143, 148, 150, 166, 167
Marriott-Dodington, Thomas 146, 151

Martin 18, 20, 71
Martinstown 25, 33, 82, 91
Matthews, Philip Wride 134
Mayo, Henry 32
McAdam, Major and Mrs 142
McEnery, Dr William 102, 142
Medlycott, Sir William 39
Melbourne, Lord 18
Melbury Bubb 149, 150
Melbury Sampford 35
Melcombe Horsey 20, 21, 29, 30, 37, 40, 41, 58, 62, 63, 67, 68, 75, 85, 91, 93, 151
Mere 8, 61
Meynell, Hugo 10
Meyrick, Mr 154
Michel, Sir John 132
Middlemarsh 32, 41, 59, 92, 134, 135, 140, 153
Milborne St Andrew 10, 15, 29-31, 33-35, 37, 38, 43, 44, 56, 58, 75, 77, 80, 81, 83, 84, 85, 87-89, 93, 94, 133
Milborne Port 39, 131, 135, 137, 145, 146, 148, 151
Miller, Michael 85, 87
Milton Abbas 10, 15, 16, 19, 20, 30, 36, 45, 63, 64, 67-69, 75, 80, 86, 88, 89, 93, 94, 95, 96, 103, 133
Minterne Magna 41, 59, 61, 92, 96, 147
Mitchel, Joe 54
Moor Crichel 15-17, 19, 31, 40, 44, 73
Monkton Up Wimborne 71
Montagu, Mrs 66
Morden 69, 74, 81, 83, 96
Moreton 20, 26, 60, 76, 86, 95
Moss, Joe 67, 71
Motcombe 131, 154
Mount Batten, Colonel 142
Mountain Harriers 57-65
Mudford 34
Munro, Miss 71
Murray, Admiral 71

Nash, Harry 63
Ness, Major 166
Nether Cerne 22, 31, 32, 41, 42, 45, 99
Newton 137
North, Dudley Francis 101
North Wootton [Dorset] 135, 144, 148, 151
North Wootton [Somerset] 139
North, Lord 101
Nottington 24
Nyland 140, 141, 143, 146, 150, 153

Okeford Fitzpaine 16, 45, 70
Onslow, Lord 149
Orbell, George 135-138, 141, 144, 146, 149, 150, 152
Orchard Portman 66
Orred, family 142
Osmington 91
Otter Hounds 169-172

Over Compton 142
Owermoigne 90
Paget, Leopold 142, 166
Paine, Admiral 39
Pamphill 20
Parke, Anna 71
Parke, Charles 82
Parke, Sir William 138
Parkinson, Joseph 66
Paul, John Domett 96
Pearce, Stephen 97
Penny, James 33, 76
Pentridge [Cranborne] 15, 31
Pentridge [Sturminster Newton] 136, 167
Pepys, Mr 133
Phelips, Charles 142
Pickard-Cambridge, family 69
Piddlehinton 20, 22, 30, 31, 38, 40, 44, 45, 57, 90, 96, 172
Piddletrenthide 19, 20, 24, 31, 32, 40, 59, 68, 84, 86, 90, 96, 125
Pimperne 15, 37
Pinford 145, 151
Place, Alfred Fox 134
Plowden, Mr and Mrs 134
Plush 35, 40, 64, 67, 68, 84-87, 132, 148
Poltimore, Baron 82, 83, 85, 99, 101, 130
Poole 69, 82
Poole, H. 133
Pope, Edward 27, 35
Porter, John 26
Portesham 8, 82, 108, 112, 113, 126
Portman, Edward Berkeley [1st Viscount] 23, 37, 46, 66-71, 74, 96, 129, 130
Portman, Henry William Berkeley [2nd Viscount] 18, 67
Portsmouth, Lord 129, 130, 133
Poundbury 21
Powerstock 20, 27, 28
Poxwell 90, 121, 122
Poyntington 137, 145
Press, John 130-133
Puddletown 15, 19, 20, 22, 27, 36, 37, 41, 57, 67, 88, 92, 94, 96
Pulham 24, 32, 33, 34, 36, 43, 62, 92, 142, 144, 149, 170
Puncknowle 20, 26, 27, 29, 83, 101
Purse Caundle 148
Puxey 23, 137

Quarleston 81
Quick, Captain 84

Radclyffe, Charles James 80-98
Rampisham 20
Ranston 166-168
Raxworthy, Mr 37
Richards, George 30
Rimpton 141, 146
Robertson, Mr 142

Rockbourne 71
Rodden 83, 99, 118
Roebuck Hounds 56
Rogers, Thomas Englesby 142

Salisbury 15, 61, 146
Sampson, Mr 25
Sandford Orcas 141
Sandford, Mr 150
Sandford, Wills 142
Sansom, Farmer 21
Satorius, Francis 11, 13
Scarsdale, Lord 47
Scobell, Captain 142
Scott, James 47
Seavington Hunt 171
Serrell, Alys F. 142, 167, 169, 170
Seward, Edwin 8, 108, 115, 118, 120
Seymer, Mr and Mrs Clay Ker 167
Seymour, C. D. 155
Shaftesbury 8, 18, 19
Shaftesbury, Lord 31, 40, 71
Shannon, Earl of 66
Sheppard, Levi 92, 93, 96
Sherborne 19, 20, 32, 32, 34, 35, 102,
135, 138, 139, 141-146, 148, 151-153,
158, 161, 164
Sheridan, Florence 99
Sheridan, Richard Brinsley 29, 99
Shillingstone 43, 70
Shilvinghampton 25, 83
Shipton Gorge 28
Shirley, Major 65
Shitterton 27
Shroton 9, 166
Simmonds, horse-dealers 89
Sixpenny Handley 19, 20
Smith, John 66
South Dorset Hounds 99-107
South Poorton 100
Spetisbury 20, 36, 81
Spinks, Mr 63
Spy, cartoon 72
Stalbridge 43, 131, 137, 138, 140, 143,
147, 149, 153
Stalbridge Weston 147
Stanley, Captain 129
Stepleton 9-12, 70
Stinsford 104
Stock Gaylard 39, 43, 54, 59, 67, 129,
142, 143, 147, 149, 152
Stoke Wake 36, 60, 62, 64, 86, 94, 151
Stour Provost 140, 167
Stourhead 54
Stourpaine 9
Stourton Caundle 138
Stowell 146
Strachey, R. 129
Stratton 21, 23, 30, 33, 41, 119, 122, 123
Stuart, John 11
Sturminster Newton 18, 20, 33, 65,
133, 136, 143, 158

Sturt, Henry Gerard 45, 87
Sturt, Humphry 15, 17, 21
Sturt, Napier 84
Surtees, Nathaniel 103, 142
Swyre 121
Sydling St Nicholas 20, 22, 28, 41, 42,
62, 92, 96, 99, 102, 109, 119, 121, 124
Symonds, Giles 102
Symonds, Henry 7, 21, 24, 26, 33, 34,
35, 37-41, 43, 46, 70, 84, 85, 87-89, 95,
96, 133
Symondsbury 171

Tadnoll 26
Tarrant Gunville 18, 24, 25, 37
Tarrant Hinton 15
Tarrant Launceston 28, 77
Taylor, Geoffrey and Joan 156
Templecombe 133, 146, 151
Thornhill 43, 138, 147, 149
Thornford 19, 145, 149, 150
Thornicombe 15, 53, 81
Throop 27, 94, 95
Thynne, Lord Harry 129
Tincleton 15, 26, 27, 38, 76, 86, 94, 95,
106
Todber 18, 167
Toller Fratrum 109
Toller Porcorum 27, 109
Tolpuddle 29, 35-39, 77, 80, 84, 85, 88,
94, 95
Tracy, Mr Courtenay 170
Treadwell, Charles 47
Treadwell, James 'Jem' 20, 24, 26, 28-
32, 34, 35, 37, 38, 40-43, 45-47, 53, 86,
87, 101
Treadwell, Tom 47
Trent 141, 147
Trigon 70
Troy Town 92
Troyte-Bullock, William 8
Tudway, Mr 47
Turners Puddle 27
Turnworth 20, 44, 45, 56, 70
Tyrwhitt-Drake, Frederick 142

Uddens 20, 31
Up Cerne 20, 41, 42, 61, 92, 96, 112,
141, 147, 153
Upwey 22, 24, 25, 27, 91, 110, 111, 117

Vansittart, Mr 36
Verwood 18
Villebois, Mr 130

Waddon 8, 91
Waller, William 142
Walton Elm 148
Wareham 60, 70, 84
Warmwell 20, 26, 57, 90
Waterston 22, 30, 33, 35, 38, 45, 57,
76, 88, 95, 96, 100

Weatherby, Mr 145
Wells 47, 168
West Compton 25-27
West Knighton 26, 59, 91
West Parley 18
West Stafford 26, 33, 38, 57, 58
West Stour 168
Westminster, Marquess and
Marchioness of 131, 154
Weymouth 8, 22, 24-27, 30, 38, 39,
104, 110, 168
Whatcombe 15, 36, 56, 69, 75, 85, 88
Whieldon, George 34, 129
Whitcombe 91, 105, 106
Whyte-Melville, Major 166, 168
Williams, E. W. 102
Williams, Mr 42
Wimborne 19, 20, 45, 82
Wimborne St Giles 40, 71
Wincanton 129, 142, 156
Winfrith Newburgh 26, 30, 90
Winterborne Came 38, 59, 90, 91
Winterborne Clenston 81
Winterborne Houghton 36, 39, 44, 45,
56, 63, 70, 87
Winterborne Kingston 29, 45, 69, 81, 83
Winterborne Monkton 27, 91
Winterborne St Martin 25
Winterborne Stickland 44, 67, 81
Winterborne Whitechurch 15, 30, 36,
39, 69, 75, 77, 81, 83, 84, 88, 89, 93, 95
Winterborne Zelston 96
Winterbourne Abbas 25, 42
Winterbourne Steepleton 20, 22, 24,
25, 82, 100, 101
Winyard's Gap 20, 116
Wolverton, Baron and Baroness 166-168
Woodsford 58
Woodyates 31, 40
Wool 20, 26, 60
Woolland 36, 62, 63, 64, 65, 68, 87, 91,
151
Worgret 84
Wrackleford 118, 119, 124
Wraxall 116, 120
Wynford Eagle 20, 25, 28, 100
Wynn, Sir Watkin 130, 154
Wytherstone 20, 27, 28, 100

Yarlington 142
Yeatman, Harry Farr 54, 55, 58, 59,
68, 69, 129, 133
Yeovil 20, 42, 44, 54, 141
Yenston 156
Yetminster 19-21, 145
Young, Mr 83

Zeals 8
Zelston 96